MAKE

WORLD

Morning Zen

Natasha, enjoy & remember

" Empower Your Life by Transforming Your Mornings '

Achroi
13/may/22

MORNING ZEN

Empower Your Life

by Transforming Your Mornings

ADRIAN GONZALEZ

© 2022 **Europe Books**| London

www.europebooks.co.uk | info@europebooks.co.uk

ISBN 9791220118620

First edition: March 2022

Distribution for the United Kingdom: **Vine House Distribution ltd**

Printed for Italy by Rotomail Italia

Finito di stampare presso Rotomail Italia S.p.A. - Vignate (MI)

Dedicated to my mom,

hope you feel proud.

MY THANKS

First, I would like to thank God, who gave me the talent and carried me through all these experiences so I could share them in this book.

Next, I would like to thank you for taking the time to read this book, being ready to embark on a powerful journey.

My objective is to share my more than ten years of experience with Morning Zen so everybody, including you, can use this practice in their daily lives and build on it, shaping ourselves into a better way of living.

Life is about learning and sharing, defined into two main actions: giving and receiving. By getting this book, you are performing both. Thank you and let's enjoy the ride.

Life is 10% what happens to me
and 90% how I wake up in the morning.

DISCLAIMER

All the information and characteristics in this book are based on the author's point of view. This information is not intended as a substitute for professional medical advice. Don't use this information to diagnose or develop a treatment plan for a health problem or disease. If you need medical attention, please seek for professional medical assistance immediately. Neither the publisher nor the author shall be liable for any physical, health, psychological, emotional, financial, personal, or commercial damage.

This book is designed to provide information and positive motivation to the readers. The information contained in this book are the author's experiences, therefore if you wish to apply these ideas, experiences or practices contained in this book, you are taking full responsibility for your actions.

PREFACE

We incorporate new things into our lives when we think deeply about them, reflect on them, practice them, and share them. So, whenever you feel like this while reading this book, it means new connections are forming in your brain. Neurons are regenerating, and intelligence is taking place, so it's okay to pause and be present. Reflect on new concepts, learn them, give them a shot, and incorporate them into your daily routine, and you will see that the rest will be fun.

INTRODUCTION

Morning Zen is a series of seamless habits that has been structured to be performed in your mornings. The catch is, within the progress of performing them, you will understand a new meaning of success.

For better life integration, this set of habits has been divided into three blocks. The first block contains three habits, the second another five, very easy to perform, while in the third and final block the last three.

We suggest integrating a block per week. Meaning, first week, first block. Second week, first block plus second block. And the third week, the sequence of the three blocks continuously.

With this said, we are ready to start and:

Welcome to Morning Zen.

CHAPTER 1

ARGUE WITH

THE EXPERIENCE

Morning Zen

Adrian Gonzalez

Instagram: @the_morning_zen

CHAPTER 1

ARGUE WITH THE EXPERIENCE

"Don't just talk; argue with the experience."

Many people practice great habits, like going to the gym, meditating, etc., but they cannot incorporate them into a long-term routine. Well, let me tell you that once you finish this book, you will start a new process, one that will help you understand the origin of habits so you can wire your brain to include them in your daily routine and prepare yourself for the day's battle.

Once you understand why some habits stick while others don't, it becomes much easier to establish them. Sometimes we practice habits because we know they are good, but we don't go behind the scenes and deeply research the reason why we should do them. Consequently, the practice doesn't stick in our brains.

I'm Panamanian, born and raised. I love eating ho-jaldre, watching soccer (La Liga Española), hitting the weights at the gym, and reviewing study cases from the Harvard Business School. But my greatest passion all these years is arguing points of view based on my lived experiences.

In short, I like to "argue with the experience." When sitting in a BBQ grill on a Sunday afternoon, discussing a specific subject with your pals, the person with the best card on the table is the one who has lived it, especially if they've experienced its complete journey.

For example, while living in Argentina, I used to go out some Sundays in search of good pizza in the city. Then, on Mondays, I'd tell my coworkers and friends about the nice pizza I'd enjoyed at a specific restaurant, and they would always jump in and say, "Well, the best pizza is from this other restaurant." It was difficult to discuss the topic with them because I hadn't visited that restaurant nor tasted the pizza they'd suggested. So, I thought to myself, what can I do to avoid this lack of knowledge about pizza? Why was there always a pizza restaurant that I had missed? Was there a list? Maybe I should do a pizza tour, visiting all these popular restaurants that my friends had recommended. Then, I could explain in great detail what my top pizza in the city was. After tasting all of them, I could share my experiences with them. So, I began to prepare myself for this journey called the Pizza Tour.

When my brother, Arkel, flew into town to visit me, we talked about it and decided to make it more like a competition. By the way, Arkel is one of the best doctors I know, and I will tell you why later in this book.

Returning to the story, first, we embarked on a three-day adventure, eating nothing but pizza.

For our guide, we used a list mentioned in a short TV commercial for Banco Ciudad de Argentina. The bank has a great advertising campaign that says, "You already know your city, right? Now know your bank." This campaign is awesome because the ads mention local things, traditions, and jokes that only Porteños know (Porteños are people born in Buenos Aires). This particular commercial focused on the best pizza in the city. As a matter of fact, you can find this video on YouTube. Just type "Banco Ciudad Pizza," and you will know what I mean (or go to the Instagram bio link @the_morning_zen).

By the end of our journey, we had determined the top pizza places in the city. And of course, after tasting the

11th slice, we started to appreciate other properties of this Italian dish, like the difference in freshness, quality of the crust, and the ingredients used to make it. It was hard to decide which pizzas qualified and which were off the list, but in the end, we made our selections, and we had a much greater understanding of artisan pizza. What do I mean by this?

Well, artisan pizza quality depends on the ingredients. They need to be fresh, correct, and ready to be enjoyed by the diner. Consequently, they are not like the big pizza chains, where, to maintain the same taste, quality, and economy of scale, the majority of the ingredients have to come from headquarters. By this, I'm not saying these big chains don't deliver delicious pizza, because they do. But we need to compare apples to apples.

Artisan pizza depends on local ingredients that are grown and harvested with local water, earth, and breeze. This type of pizza has a local stamp to its ingredients that makes it unique. And this not only applies to pizza places but to the majority of local restaurants. So, if you have the opportunity to visit a new city, ask around for artisanal local restaurants; you will definitely enjoy the experience of eating at one. In other words, besides knowing this new city, you will also know its flavor.

Back to the story. At the end of the journey, and sated with pizza for days, we finally selected a winner. For us, they made the best artisanal pizza in Buenos Aires and— why not—in the world. Well, I have been to several pizza capitals, including Chicago, with its famous deep-dish pizzas, New York City, Rome, and Catania, as well as local restaurants in Italy, and in my opinion, Buenos Aires, Argentina has several of the best pizza restaurants in the world. That being said, if you want me to try a good artisan pizza restaurant, please contact me, and I will be glad to visit, taste, and compare.

Well, the place with the most amazing pizza is located in the center of Buenos Aires, between Talcahuano Street and Marcelo T, and is named El Cuartito. If you have the opportunity to visit Buenos Aires, please go to El Cuartito. Ask for the "Fugazzetta Rellena con Jamón y Morrón", which has grilled cubes of mozzarella, little slices of onions, ham, and red peppers, all perfectly baked. Two words: the BEST.

I know tastes are a personal thing, but since that day, I've come to understand that the best way to know about something is to try it, compare it, and share your experience with others. And this is what is this book about.

For the last few years, I have been testing and

researching many different things in life so I can provide my point of view based on my experience on that topic, so I have lived both sides of the coin and understand the how and why of things.

In other words, I have been arguing with the experience, and this is what I will share with you in these next chapters, my experience and why we should transform our mornings, so you can understand what I mean by the new meaning of success.

CHAPTER 2

THE NEW MEANING

OF SUCCESS

Morning Zen

Adrian Gonzalez

Instagram: @the_morning_zen

CHAPTER 2

THE NEW MEANING OF SUCCESS

In this book, you will begin to understand success is not the act of achieving what you are pursuing. In other words, it is not acquiring what we want because we fought so hard and pushed through till we got it. It is so much more than that.

I invite you to discover the other meaning of success: accomplishing all your daily habits under your control. And these morning habits will be part of a new transformation.

In his book *Chasing Excellence*, Ben Bergeron describes the mindset of two amazing athletes, passing through the toughest competition that exists right now, the World CrossFit Games. (If you have the chance, read this book. Two words: highly recommended.)

As Ben explains, we experience two types of situations every day: those we can control and those we can't.

For these elite athletes, excellence is successfully completing a task, training session, or commitment, all things they can control, and they do not put energy into what they cannot control.

The Icelandic athlete Katrin Davidsdottir defines success with these words: "We choose to focus on what's inside our control, and what we can control is exactly what defines as success."

In 2016, the year Ben Bergeron wrote his book, Katrin Davidsdottir and Mat Fraser won the CrossFit Games, earning the titles of fittest woman and man on Earth.

Success is what we can focus on this day, this hour, this minute, so focus on completing all these amazing habits for Morning Zen, and you will conquer your morning, your day.

What happens during the day, problems, situations, pending tasks, are part of daily life, and most of them are things you cannot control. Remember, these habits will be under your control, and if you complete them, you will succeed for the day. That is what I call success.

To fully enjoy this book, I recommend practicing Morning Zen as you read. Yes, put the process into practice right now.

Many people, including me, like to read everything first and then use what we think is most important. And guess what? Most of the time, we do not do it. We read the book, close it, and never open it again.

This book is different. It has been designed so you can start practicing Morning Zen on day one and as you read it. So focus on now, on the moment, on the present.

When you complete this book, you will say, "Adrian was right. The magic of this book is that I can incorporate and practice Morning Zen while I read it." So, start it now. Don't wait until next Monday, like the eternal diet we always want to begin but never start. Let's avoid procrastination and, with no regrets, start now—yes, right now.

So, to warm up and put into action what this book is about, I will tell you the first three steps to start Morning Zen. And you may ask, "Do I have to wake up earlier?" The answer is YES, but no worries. We will explain the why and how much time will be needed.

The first three steps are: wake up with no alarm, drink the Morning Concoction, and perform Collected Conscious Breathing.

For Morning Zen to work, you need to disconnect from the outside world and focus on yourself, your capsule, and your home. No TV nor cellphones are allowed until Morning Zen ends. And by no cellphone, I mean no email, no social networks, no news, no text messages, and no communication apps. Forget about the world for a moment because this is your precious time, by and for you.

As a matter of fact, once you start practicing Morning Zen, you will soon learn that most people are getting ready to start their day, so there will be not much that cannot wait a couple of minutes till you finish.

The first thing you need to do is wake up 35 minutes before your usual time. This means, if you wake up at 7:00 am, you will need to start waking up at 6:25. Or if you usually wake up at 6:30, now you will start waking up at 5:55. This does not mean you are in Robin Sharma's 5 AM Club, an interesting book written by a great writer. (By the way, Robin, if you are reading this book, I send you my sincere greetings.)

With this, you will have a new routine that will consume more minutes than your regular one, so it's necessary to wake up earlier. And since this is a new schedule, you will need an alarm to wake you up.

Consequently, there is something you should get or buy so you can start working on this process flawlessly, unless you already have one in your room. And yes, we are still making sure that the first thing you do in the morning is NOT to grab your cellphone, because, once you pick it up, you will start surfing on it and then you will connect to your outside world, and right now, we want to do the opposite. We want a dedicated time, by us and for us, with a deep connection with our inner world.

So, what is that thing we must get or buy? Well, it's nothing less than a digital table clock. Why do we need one? Because every time we open our eyes, the first thing we want to know is what time it is. Even though we set the alarm, we still want to double-check the time.

So, what about the people who wake up with no alarm? And do people who snooze want to see what time it is? Well, for both questions, the answer is yes. Believe it or not, the first thing most of us do in the morning is checking what time it is. But what happens if your alarm is on your cellphone? Then the first thing you do when you wake up is to grab it, and once you have it in your hands, you're tempted to check your messages and everything else, breaking the rule and habit of no cellphone till Morning Zen ends.

So, buy/get a digital clock. It can be a cheap one; it doesn't have to be expensive, or state of the art. Remember to buy it with batteries in case there is a power outage.

Where should it go? Most of the time, we put the digital clock on the nightstand, just beside us, and that is an error because it comes with the temptation to start hitting the snooze button. Why? Because the alarm is only an arm's length away. Hence, if you have the alarm on your nightstand, I recommend moving it right away. Besides, if you like to hit the snooze button or have multiple alarms, let me tell you that this is more negative than positive.

I recommend you stop snoozing and use just one alarm. That alarm should lead to just one reaction: jumping out of bed to turn it off, so the best place to set your digital clock is on a table in front of your bed.

This has two benefits. One is, once you open your eyes, you will be able to see what time it is without having to turn your head. The second is that to shut it down, you will have to get out of bed, walk a couple of steps, and turn it off. And with this little hike, believe me, you will wake up.

Why digital? Because our brains are lazy, and if you use an analog clock, sometimes you have to think about what time it is, which can be difficult after a nice sleep in a relaxing bed. So, make it easy for your brain and go digital.

You may be asking, "Adrian, what about the people who wake up with no alarm?" Well, that is a great habit that we will learn more about in the next chapter. But because this is a new process and we will start incorporating a new schedule, we will need to use the support of an alarm until we establish the habit of waking up on our own.

So, the first thing to do is go to Amazon or the nearest local store and buy a digital clock to put in front of your bed. Then set the alarm for 35 minutes before your regular wake-up time.

To better understand the how and why of waking up with no alarm, join me in the next chapter, "The Morning Battle." I'm certain you will like it.

CHAPTER 3

THE MORNING

BATTLE

Morning Zen

Adrian Gonzalez

Instagram: @the_morning_zen

CHAPTER 3

THE MORNING BATTLE

"A great morning starts with a great last night."

–Adrian Gonzalez

Prepare for your morning with no interruptions. By this, I mean, turn your cellphone off or put it in airplane or do-not-disturb mode when you go to sleep.

Nowadays, most phones have this setting, and you can program the do-not-disturb period to last from when you go to sleep until you finish your Morning Zen.

And in case you don't know how to do it, just put this book on hold, pull up Google, and search how to set the do-not-disturb schedule.

Worst case scenario, turn off your phone, put it on silent or airplane mode until Morning Zen is finished.

It is important to let your favorite people know, they shouldn't call you during this period, and I will explain how to do this.

First, make a list from the top of your head of your inner circle, and by that, I mean all the important people who, no matter what, you will answer their call. For example, your inner circle might include your wife, husband, significant other, mother, father, boss, son, daughter, best friend, business partners, secretary, assistant, messenger, anyone whose call may be very important.

Once you've made the list, contact them one by one and explain to them that you are in the process of incorporating new habits early in the morning and, to accomplish them, you need full concentration, so you would appreciate it if they could please avoid contacting you until a specific time (in this case, when your Morning Zen finishes). After that time, you will be more than happy to attend any call or communication. For example, I finish my Morning Zen at 7:45 am, so everyone in my inner circle knows that I will only respond to calls, chats, or emails after that time.

As I said, it is important they understand you will be unavailable during the first hours of the morning. They need to respect this time, and please, if they have to call, it should be because the sky is falling. Believe me, once you communicate this, they will understand.

So, start right away and make this list, and then send them a voice note so they get the message. This helps to avoid turning your note into a 30-minute conversation with each person. And with the help of technology, you just have to record the voice note once and forward it to the rest of your list. This will take you 15 minutes of your time.

Why a voice note? Because people can better understand the tone of messages when they hear the person's voice rather than read a text message, particularly when it's saying something like, "Please don't call me in the morning till XX: XX am." Once you've accomplished this task, the rest of the world can wait until you finish your Morning Zen.

The first habit I'm going to explain so you can officially start your Morning Zen is waking up early with no alarm. By this, I am not saying that you have to get rid of the wake-up alarms in your life.

I still use the alarm if I have to get up at a different

time than usual, like for an early-morning flight or if I need to wake up from a power nap. But the habit of waking up early with no alarm is something you will need to start developing in the next few days, and I will tell you why.

Have you ever met someone who said, "I wake up every morning with no alarm," or, "I have an internal clock. I always wake up when I want to with no alarm." Well, believe it or not, your body is a perfect machine that tells you when you are tired, hungry, sick, or energized, so, why can't it also tell you when it would be a great time to wake up in the morning?

And that is true; you can wake up on time and with no alarm.

I started investigating the sleep process a long time ago, so allow me to explain it a little bit more. We go through several stages of sleep, and the optimal one is the famous "deep sleep." The bad news is most of us are unable to stay in that stage naturally for more than 30 minutes, so I asked myself, "If this is the best part of sleeping, why can't we stay there longer?" I started to "argue with the experience," experimenting with my body to crack this code and extend this deep sleep.

The American Academy of Sleep Medicine classifies

sleep as consisting of 4 stages. The first stage is falling asleep, the second stage is light sleep, the third one is deep sleep, and the fourth is REM. And no, it is not the famous American band from Athens, Georgia, that sings the '90s hit "Losing My Religion." Well, as a matter of fact, they got the name of the band from this famous sleep stage, but the acronym REM means rapid eye movement.

We will focus on three of these stages, the most important ones. They are light sleep, deep sleep, and REM. Let me explain them further.

Light sleep occurs once you fall asleep, meaning the classic first couple of minutes you are in the sleeping process, when you notice any light sound that reaches your ears. That is why the stage is named "light sleep": you are sleeping lightly.

Then comes deep sleep, when you are fully disconnected, almost like a steady, heavy rock, like you are dead, making this stage the one where we rest the most.

Last is the REM stage, which is where our brain liberates key emotional and memory-related structures, turning them into dreams. When someone's eyeballs move while they are sleeping, it means they are in the REM stage and should be dreaming. As we sleep, we pass through these different stages, and each one of them lasts no more than 30 minutes. This means that you will stay less than 30 minutes in each stage, and then the cycle loops again.

That is why sometimes we can wake up from just a little noise far away, like falling silverware in the kitchen, while, other times, there could be an earthquake, and we would not even notice it.

And that is the magic of our body. While sleeping, sometimes we need to have the radar on for anything that could happen during the night, and sometimes we need to be fully disconnected to be well rested.

And then there is the famous power nap. In case you have not heard about it, let me explain. The power nap is a short sleep you can take during the day or after lunch, where the objective is to have a quick recovery or revitalization.

This power nap should not be longer than 30 minutes, because then you will jump from light sleep to deep sleep, and once you cross that stage, it will be harder for you to get up. This means that, if you set the alarm past 30 minutes, sleep into the next stage, and suddenly wake up, there is a high probability that when you get up, you will feel tired or disoriented as a result of waking up in the deep sleep stage.

As a matter of fact, NASA recommends that the power nap should be no more than 27 minutes.

So, to summarize, a power nap is a short little siesta, no more than 27 minutes, that gives you a little bit of recovery or energy boost, and it takes place in the light sleep stage.

Getting back in the topic, when you complete a round of sleep, passing through these three stages, and start all over again, that is what we call a cycle. For example, you complete a cycle when you pass through light sleep, deep sleep, REM, deep sleep, and back to light sleep.

And as I mentioned before, each stage can last no more than 30 minutes, which means, a complete cycle should take you approximately one hour and 30 minutes. It can last a few minutes more or a few minutes less, but on average, it takes 1.5 hours. And now comes the famous question: "How many hours should I sleep?"

Before we get into that, let me tell you about a question I had as I studied sleep stages: what can I do to make deep sleep last longer so I can feel more rested when I wake up?

Well, let me tell you I began researching all the possibilities to make this happen, because, if I could make the deep-sleep stage last more than 30 minutes, I could rest more, recharge better, and optimize my sleep. While on this journey, I found several practices for doing so.

One of them was a sleep diet. A sleep diet? Hahaha, yes, I was in shock as well. As we all know, there are food diets, where the objective is to control the amount of food ingested in terms of calories, proteins, fats, and carbs. Well, there is also a sleep diet, but no worries; it has nothing to do with food.

So, I started investigating these Sleep diets, and I discovered that their objective is to tire your body with your regular journey while controlling and scheduling your sleep time. You may say, "Well, I do that already. I have a time to go to bed and a time to wake up." But it's not like that. It's more like sleeping less during the sleeping process so, when it comes time for real sleep, your body will be so tired that you will fall like a brick and your deep sleep stage will be longer.

There is an extreme sleep diet called the 2-2-20, which consists of sleeping deeply for two hours. During the rest of the day, every two hours, you have to sleep for 20 minutes. In part, you are getting several shots of light sleep, but when it comes to the two hours of sleep, you will spend more of that time in deep sleep.

From the accounts of people who have tried it, it seems very painful, and the worst part is that when it comes to your 20 minutes of sleep, you have to take it because you are waiting for it. So, if you are on a date or in a meeting, you have to stop what you are doing, leave everything, find a comfortable place to sleep, and lose them for 20 minutes while they wait for you to appear again. For most people, this schedule is very difficult to follow.

I made the 4x2, which means four hours two times a day, part of my journey. You may ask, "How did you put this into practice?" Well, I started by sleeping two times a day. How do I do that? Well, instead of sleeping eight hours at night, I slept four hours at night and four hours after work.

It sounds complicated, but if you like math, it's almost the same. We have 24 hours a day, and we sleep eight of those, leaving 16 hours for the rest of our daily tasks. Therefore, I started by practicing, sleeping four hours before work and four hours after returning from the office, and I still had the same 16 hours for the rest of my day.

To be more specific, I went to sleep at 3:00 am and woke up at 7:00 am (four hours), did my morning routine, ate breakfast, got ready for work, went to the office, worked from 9:00 to 5:00, went back home, and went back to bed at 6:00 pm for the next four hours.

I woke up at 10:00 pm, ate dinner, went to the gym, hit the weights from 11:00 pm to 12:00 am, went back home, showered, and drank my protein shake. From 12:50 am to 2:50 am, I did stuff like taking care of pending work, reading a book, or seeing a movie, and then I went back to sleep at 3:00 am.

By the way, I was single at the time, with no children, and yes, it was kind of a selfish life, but I enjoyed it. And in case I wanted to go out for dinner, I scheduled my dates and commitments for 10:30 pm, which, in places like Spain and Argentina, is a normal time to go out for dinner. I did the rest of my stuff during the weekend, when I maintained the same sleep schedule so it did not break into my weekly routine.

You may be asking, "Did it work?" Well, I felt rested and had a lot of energy. Indeed, I felt more energized than a normal person. I could focus well, do my things, and did not feel tired at all.

The catch was that it was like a boost. This meant that

ADRIAN GONZALEZ

after sleeping for four hours, I felt fresh, full, and loaded with energy for the next several hours. The bad news was, when the 11th hour passed, my body automatically shut down no matter where I was.

Thus, if I was on the subway at 6:30 pm, my body would shut down and enter sleep mode while I was standing there, holding onto the bar attached to the ceiling of the subway car.

So, if you are asking how a person could sleep on the subway while standing with one hand clinging to a bar, well, maybe he is on a 4x2 sleep diet, or maybe he has not slept for days, or maybe that person was me.

You may also be asking, "How long did you do it?" The answer is a couple of months, but then I had to fly back to Panama for the holidays, and I had to drop it. But on the bright side, it helped me understand how the sleep process works.

Consequently, as I was explaining, a complete sleep-stage cycle can take around an hour and a half. This means that if you sleep six hours a day, you are completing four cycles, and if you sleep eight hours a day, you are completing five cycles.

You may ask, "Which one is better?" And the response

is, both are ok. Just use the one that works for you and you are used to. When we were at school, my brother only rested for six hours a day, from 12:00 am to 6:00 am, and today, when he's 44 years old, happily married with two children, he still sleeps six hours a day, or four cycles, and it works perfectly for him. The important thing is that you complete the cycles, at least four of them, so you feel ready for the day when you wake up. As for me, I do four cycles and take a power nap during the day.

The best part of waking when the cycle is completed is that you can wake up with no alarm. And that is part of the FIRST HABIT of Morning Zen: **waking up with no alarm**. When you understand this, you can better program your sleep at night. Determine how many cycles you want to sleep and start waking up with no alarm.

As I said before, we have to reprogram a new wake-up time, and to start Morning Zen, we need to wake up at least 35 minutes before our regular time. So, do the math, start going to bed at a time that lets you complete four or five cycles, depending on what you are used to, and wake up with no alarm according to your new schedule. Practice it until you get it.

You might be asking, "What are the benefits of waking up with no alarm?" Well, when you wake up on your own, you tell your body that you are ready to start the day, that you are fresh, and you will feel the energy you need. You are in control of your body, not an alarm that wakes you up because you are tired or lazy. Wake up naturally, and you will vibe to the world that you are ready for your new day, one with good things to come.

The next process, which is very important, is when you are about to go to sleep. Take a moment to repeat in your mind several times the exact time you want to wake up. And it will start working. Remember that we have an internal clock, and if you repeat to yourself several times when you want to wake up, bang! You will.

What about the real clock alarm? Well, I recommend using that alarm for the first few days as a backup for waking up. For example, let's say you set your mind to wake up at 6:00 a.m. Well, you can set the alarm as a backup to wake you up at 6:10 a.m., but it will be a "just in case" alarm. Remember that the new habit we are incorporating is waking up with no alarm, so you should be loyal to yourself and not rely on the backup alarm to get up.

As I said before, set your internal bio alarm by repeating the time you want to wake up, and you will see that you will wake up one to four minutes before the time you set in your mind. Wake up and start your day. Try it. Trust me, it works. If not, ask Oprah Winfrey. Yes, she does it as well.

An article from *Career Girl Daily*, written by Beth Mourato and titled "How to Plan Your Day Like Oprah Winfrey," explains how Oprah Winfrey relies on her internal clock to wake up by herself at the optimal time, and from there, her day starts. Oprah, if you are reading this, my greetings.

Now you may be asking, "Why the digital table clock?" Well, instead of grabbing your phone, it will be the first thing you check when you wake up to see if you are late for the day while practicing this new habit, and it's a backup for our first Morning Zen habit, waking up with no alarm.

So, to close this chapter, start right now. Get that digital clock, put it in the appropriate spot, and set the time to go to bed. Repeat to yourself several times when you want to wake up, and the next morning, when you get up, check the time on the digital clock. And if it is the time you set in your mind the night before, Morning Zen is already working. After that, jump from the bed, start your day, and proceed with the Kitchen Lab, which is explained in the next chapter.

The best thing is that by completing this first habit daily, you are already starting your morning with energy, winning the morning battle with the easy and natural practice of waking up with no alarm.

So, go ahead and wake up with no alarm and then join me in the next chapter, which explains the next healthy habit, the Kitchen Lab.

CHAPTER 4

THE KITCHEN

LAB

Morning Zen

Adrian Gonzalez

Instagram: @the_morning_zen

CHAPTER 4

THE KITCHEN LAB

The second habit in Morning Zen is the juice you will prepare in your Kitchen Lab, or as other people like it to call it, the Morning Concoction. And what is this Morning Concoction habit? Well, it works like this. As soon as you wake up with no alarm, deactivate the backup alarm. Then, go to the kitchen and prepare or have ready that special morning juice that will support a healthy diet and, therefore, a better life. You have to drink this juice without eating anything so your body can absorb it better.

And what can it be? Well, you can use wheatgrass, lemon water, apple vinegar, and a mix of antioxidants, accompanied with extras, such as raw honey, garlic, ginger, etc. Include what suits you or integrate what you are already taking. Or do the opposite: use something you've always wanted to try but have never had the opportunity to. Now is your chance.

If you were wondering, it cannot include coffee or branded tea because they are more like breakfast drinks. That is why it is called a concoction: the idea is that it is a mix of natural, healthy things that will help you, and you want it to be the first thing your body absorbs for the day.

If you are asking, "Adrian, what is your Morning Concoction?" Well, it is easy. I use hot water, lime, and sodium bicarbonate. How much and why?

Well, I am not as famous as Ramsey Gordon, but I will give you the recipe for free.

Take a glass, add two fingers of water, and put it in the microwave for 22 seconds. (In case you don't use microwave, then, heat water on the stove.) After that, take a lime, wash it, and split it in two. Squeeze each side into the glass of warm water. Then, with the same knife that you cut lime, scoop up all the sodium bicarbonate that you can get with the tip of the knife. Pour it into the glass and stir. You will notice that the bicarbonate is reacting with the lime. This is because one is acid the other is base, but no worries; after ten seconds, it will calm down. Once it's settled, take it like a tequila shot, bottoms up and with no regrets. Voilà.

And in case you are asking, "Why of this concoction?" Well, let me share some of the benefits. One of them is that lime is rich in vitamin C and works as an antioxidant for our body. It also works as a diuretic, and if you suffer from stomach acid like me, the bicarbonate will work flawlessly as a treatment for it. Bicarbonate also alkalizes the body, bringing all the benefits that come with that.

As it happens, an article posted in *Business Insider*, written by Carlos Ferrer-Bonsoms Cruz, explains the detailed benefits of this elixir:

Healthier skin. Thanks to the vitamin C that limes contain, which gives them antioxidant properties, you will achieve better-looking skin. Among other benefits, you can fight acne, reduce the signs of aging, whiten your nails, and exfoliate your skin.

Weight loss: Although weight loss is not causally related to baking soda and lemon, baking soda is known to make you more active by giving your metabolism a boost. Therefore, if you are moving, it will be easier for you to lose weight. Although it is not the perfect solution, it helps you achieve your weight-loss goals.

Better digestion: If you drink a glass of water with these two products, you will have better digestion, which will help you avoid stomach pains or annoying gas that does not want to come out. Thanks to its fantastic benefits, your digestive system will work much better, and you will have fewer problems after a heavy meal or anything that does not sit well with you.

Better immune system: It is well known that limes can prevent diseases in the intestine. This, added to the antacid solution that sodium bicarbonate provides, will help you maintain healthy body levels so no disease can develop.

Elimination of toxins. Thanks to the diuretic properties of limes, you will be able to rid the body of excess toxins, salts, water, and fats. It is for this reason that fruit is a great ally of the kidneys. In addition, the Spanish Association of Pediatrics points out that it is exceptionally good at preventing stones in the kidney and protecting against urolithiasis.

Stronger heart. In addition to all the above benefits, Sodium bicarbonate will help you reduce "bad" cholesterol and the risk of cardiovascular problems. In addition, thanks to the combination of lime with this product, you will be able to reduce the risk of cardiovascular problems.

Due to all these benefits and more, this is the Morning Concoction that I prepare for my Morning Zen. I recommend it, so if you want to try it, go ahead. As you can see, it is very easy and practical, and it comes with all the health benefits.

If you want to do another concoction, that is ok, too. Try it and test it; that is why it is called the Kitchen Lab. But remember that the main benefit is that the drink is for your health and is part of a new habit you are incorporating into your mornings.

And guess what? The hidden benefit of this habit is that by going to the kitchen, you had to walk there, and once you are there, preparing your Morning Concoction, you are moving. That all helps you finish waking up.

Some of you might be asking, "Can I include vitamin pills in this part of Morning Zen? Well, when I test a mix of vitamins with nothing in the stomach, it gives me a stomachache. That's why I lean towards something that includes natural ingredients, such as lime.

So, now that you are waking up with no alarm, going right to the kitchen to prepare your Morning Concoction, and doing all of this without grabbing your phone, it may surprise you to know that you have started your Morning Zen process. And all of this comes with a little bit of cell-phone detox. You will feel better because you are incorporating new beneficial steps in your mornings, and you will immediately start to notice this improved sense of well-being before your nine-to-five workday begins, giving you the sensation that you are already winning.

And to close this first block of Morning Zen, you should read the next chapter, which talks about Collected Conscious Breathing. Once you read it, you will understand the why of this practice, and you will discover another focus of this habit.

So, go ahead and enjoy the next chapter.

Adrian's Morning Concoction Recipe

- Pour 2 fingers of water inside a glass.

- Put it in the microwave for 22 seconds.

- Take 1 lime, cut it in 2 and squeeze it into the glass that has the warm water.

- Sodium Bicarbonate, immerse a tip of a knife and add it to the lime warm water.

- Stir it up.

- Let it rest for 10 seconds.

- Drink it.

CHAPTER 5

COLLECTED

CONSCIOUS

BREATHING

Morning Zen

Adrian Gonzalez

Instagram: @the_morning_zen

CHAPTER 5

COLLECTED CONSCIOUS BREATHING

We are now ready for the third step, which I call Collected Conscious Breathing. Why this name? Well, it comes from constant research into how the human body works.

We'll start with stress and let me explain it this way. Stress is a survival state of mind, where cortisol, adrenaline, and other hormones are dispersed to help us cope with threats and danger. During this mode, we enter a fight-or-flight state where we can make fast decisions. Adrenaline flows into our bloodstream, giving us a boost of power and triggering all types of "ready to react" modes so we can survive.

This is not all bad. On the bright side, stress is something that helps us be focused, ready, and alert. But what happens if we don't use it? What happens if we don't liberate that energy? Well, guess what? We start accumulating it little by little until we become ill. In fact, Cortisol suppresses our immune system. That is why doctors will often say, "We verified your results, and everything looks normal, so we think it could be caused by stress," or you will hear in the office hallway, "He got sick, and they say it was because of stress."

And why does this happen? Well, go back to pre-historic times, when the caveman was outside his cave, looking to chase down some food for him and his family and, from out of nowhere, a hungry lion sneaks up on him. Guess what mode his body entered? Correct, the stress mode. Its benefits helped him to survive very real physical danger.

Nowadays, we have a more sedentary life. Most of us work in front of a computer or sit at a workstation for six to ten hours a day. Then, out of the blue, we receive a burn notice, and bang, we enter the mode of the caveman trying to survive. The difference is that the caveman uses and releases all this energy to react quickly to the threat, deal with it, and survive.

We might react to what we're facing, or sometimes overreact, but most of the time, we just suck all these feelings, hormones, and thoughts directly into our body and search for a drink or cigarette to drown out or balance them.

But mentally, what is stress? If we take a deep look, it is the constant thinking about a problem that pounds in our head until we find the solution and get things under control. So, a situation presents itself, the news enters our brain, and we start comparing our values, responsibilities, name, and reputation with the bar that has already been set in our minds. From there, we enter stress mode, generating all these things in our body until we find a solution or the issue passed. However, it is important to realize that the constant hammering of thoughts in our head is the gasoline powering the engine of this stressed-out mode.

So, what is the opposite of stress? What is the opposite of hammering our brain with stressful thoughts? How can we stop that gasoline? What can we do to start practicing this opposite?

Well, many good habits are the opposite of this stress mode, and most people can practice them with no problem: playing sports, going to the gym, running, talking with friends, and walking in the fresh air outdoors. In any case, there are several things that we can do that are the opposite of stress, and most of them depend on going someplace or being with someone. But what if we could counter stressful thoughts without depending on others or going someplace else?

Well, the answer is we can, and it's as easy as being in an isolated place and not thinking about anything. Clear your mind and do not think. But guess what? that is not our normal state of mind. As human beings, our daily existence requires thinking and rethinking. We are always thinking about something we need to do, something that may happen, something to resolve, and this is not a bad thing; this is part of our intelligence and the regular functioning of our brain.

It works this way. If we are not focusing 100% on something, we are thinking about something else. This makes sense; our mind has been designed to function this way.

So, to think about nothing, we have to consciously do it. This means focusing 100% on it and not thinking about anything else, so we have to be in a collected state of mind.

You may ask, "Adrian, what could help us focus on not

70

thinking at all?" Well, that aid will be your breathing. Yes, focusing on our breathing keeps us present and 100% in the moment. That is why I've called this step Collected Conscious Breathing.

So, what techniques exist to help us focus on the present and our breathing? Well, one of them, the most popular one, is mindfulness. I define mindfulness as nothing more than focusing on the present and using breathing to help do it, so do not think that mindfulness is a new religion, trend, movement, or way of life. For me, it's just a tool to be used for a specific objective, a support that you can control and will make things easier for you.

Using it does not mean that you are part of a movement or in the process of a lifestyle change. It is simpler than that. It's something you will use for a specific objective. For us, it will be not focusing on anything but breathing for a specific period, and that is it.

Think of it like this. You might use Microsoft Excel as a work tool, but that does not mean that you are a finance guy, or you have dedicated your life to the accounting lifestyle. It is simply a tool you use for a specific task or automatic calculations that you need in your daily job.

So, think of mindfulness meditation as a tool to be healthier and more collected, counteract stress, and reduce anxiety. You will feel more relaxed, and all of this is aligned with Collected Conscious Breathing, or CCB.

If you are already doing this practice, congratulations. Now you just have to incorporate it in your Morning Zen.

But why mindfulness? Well, let me tell you about this Spanish doctor, a fellow in surgery at Harvard University Medical School who studies the impact of mental processes on the development of talent, ability, health, and well-being. His name is Mario Alonso Puig. Mario wrote a book in 2017 called *Take a Breath! Mindfulness*. In this book, he explains all the medical benefits of meditation. He believes that meditation is medicine and can heal the body, and he lists all the supernatural benefits that come from this practice. On the kickoff tour for his book, he talked about the experience of Herbert Benson.

Herbert Benson is a cardiologist and professor of medicine at Harvard Medical School and the director of the Benson-Henry Institute of Mind Body Medicine.

Dr. Benson was highly worried about arterial hypertension, and he discovered that his patients still had moments when they got nervous or tenser and these peaks of high blood pressure were extremely dangerous for them.

One day, he asked himself, "Could it be possible to find a way to reduce blood pressure to normal levels without using massive quantities of medications, most of which have side effects?"

At that time, modern medicine said that this was impossible. As he explained, when we are tense or stressed, we activate a part of our nervous system called the sympathetic nervous system. One of its functions is to put us in alarm mode, and as a result, it triggers high blood pressure. Dr. Benson was looking for a way to reduce activity in the sympathetic nervous system, so it would not activate so often, and his patients would be better.

Now, there was also a Swiss doctor named Walter Rudolf Hess. He was an ophthalmologist who became a researcher, winning a Nobel Prize in medicine in 1949 after discovering a structure in the brain called the diencephalon. In the diencephalon there is a nucleus, now called the anterior hypothalamus, capable of activating the opposite response, which means that it can produce a state of calm. Therefore, it can counteract the activation of the sympathetic nervous system.

He studied the effect on cats, but of course, there was no way of knowing if it applied to humans. The question was, if humans did have a similar structure, how could we activate this nucleus to produce this relaxation response in a situation where there was tension?

With this information in hand, Dr. Benson looked for a way to activate this famous core. But modern medicine said that the nucleus was so deep in the brain that there was no way to activate it.

Nevertheless, by a series of curious coincidences, a book fell into Dr. Benson's hands. It explained that the Buddhist community was able to do things with the body that seemed impossible. He noticed that they were capable of activating things in their body that could only be possible if they knew the pathway to what is now called the trophotropic nucleus of the hypothalamus.

As a result, during the '60s, Benson flew to Northern India and traveled to the Tibetan community of Dharmsala. There, at an elevation of 7,000 feet, he started making records of the monks who lived there and practiced meditation.

He knew in his bones that these monks had found a way to activate this nucleus, but he was still confused. How did they do it? All they seemed to do was close their eyes. He realized that he had to investigate this phenomenon more deeply, so he founded the Institute of Mind

Body Medicine.

He found out there are indeed very ancient practices based on the Buddha's teachings that activate certain brain centers. This, in turn, puts in motion this relaxation response, and the most important thing is that this can be applied on a day-to-day basis. So, he asked himself if there was a way to share this practice with his patients and keep track of the benefits they saw.

With this, Dr. Benson became the first person in history to keep medical records on his patients to see what happened in this meditative state of mind.

After several years, his studies were able to show that meditation promotes better health, especially in individuals with hypertension. People who meditate regularly enjoy lower stress levels, increased well-being, and even reduced blood pressure and resting heart rate.

Since then, many doctors and scientists have studied the benefits of meditation, and this practice is used more than ever these days.

Dr. Mario Alonso Puig is now a famous lecturer who works with the greatest companies in the world, and he gives seminars on leadership, communication, and health, providing medical facts and scientific results so we can be better human beings. Mario, if you are reading this, thank you for providing us with this information, and I send you my greetings. As for everyone else, if you can buy his book, *Take a Breath! Mindfulness*, I suggest you do so. Two words: highly recommended.

Now you are probably asking, "Adrian, what can I do to start practicing CCB?" Well, today everything is on the internet. I mean, you can Google "guided meditation," "mindfulness meditation" or any related words and find numerous results for this type of practice. And I will help you identify the types of guided meditations that I recommend performing in the CCB.

Some meditations are meant to put you in a relaxed state. I call them "ready to sleep" meditations, and they are great if you've had a stressful day and want to relax or are having problems sleeping at night. You will recognize these meditations because they help you relax, going through the different parts of your body until you are almost ready to sleep. They are effective, but we don't recommend them for CCB.

So, which ones do I recommend, then? Well, I suggest using the Chopra Meditations. He has several bundles, like the 21-Day Abundance Challenge, and most of them are already free on the internet. But if you want to invest in something more serious, go and buy them. (Deepak, if you are reading this, I send you my sincere greetings.)

And why Chopra Meditations? Well, the answer is because they are well structured. First, every session has a different positive life topic. Second, he explains the why of this topic and what it means in our daily life. Then he provides a Sanskrit mantra that is related to the topic of the day. And last, he proceeds with the meditation. Once you finish the meditation, he recalls the day's topic, helping you finish your meditation with a positive mindset for the rest of the day.

Two words: Highly Recommended.

I understand that some of us can be a little skeptical, but as I explained at the beginning of this book, sometimes we have to do the pizza tour to know which is the best in town. So, go ahead and try to do the entire 21-day challenge and then feel free to argue with this experience. As a matter of fact, start now. Go to your electronic device and search for this meditation kit. Try typing "[No ads] 21 days of abundance challenge Deepak Chopra." And put it in your favorites so you have it ready for CCB in Morning Zen.

By this, I'm not saying that Deepak Chopra is someone you should follow, but I have to recognize that he has been a genius at spreading his knowledge and best practices to many people on this planet. Most importantly, he is leaving a transcendent knowledge to the world. He has left his mark, his trademark, and has directly and indirectly helped millions of people all over the world with these meditations. So, if you want to get the other kits, go ahead and do it. I bought them, I used them, and they worked for me very well.

A positive thing about Morning Zen is that it is not rigid. This means it has its structure, but you do not have to do exactly what it says. For example, if you tried Chopra Meditation and think you do not connect with it, that is ok. What I recommend is to search for other meditation that does create a bond with you. Other meditations that I recommend are the ones I will list on the bio link of the Instagram account for this book, and you can practice them as many times as you want.

Besides mindfulness, Collected Conscious Breathing can be any isolation practice that you would like to focus on and feel comfortable incorporating into Morning Zen. As suggested by the name, it is any state where you are collected, conscious, and using your breathing to maintain concentration. For example, you can use positive meditation, like visualization, PNL, or complete silence meditation. Nevertheless, if you already do daily meditation or have experienced similar practices, then voilà, it will be easier for you because now you can incorporate them into CCB.

When Diego Balan, a successful entrepreneur, expert in the online ticketing business, blockchain master, and friend of mine, began practicing Morning Zen, he immediately started incorporating the Silva Method – MindValley meditation, which he was practicing already. MindValley is an education platform created by the Malaysian entrepreneur Vishen Lakhani that focuses on programs for human transformation. One of them is the Silva Ultra Mind System. This system is inspired by the book by Jose Silva, *The Silva Mind Control Method*, which focuses on personal growth and goes beyond meditation and manifesting. As an example, these types of programs can be used to provide variety to CCB. Vishen, if you are reading this, my greetings.

Thus, I am not saying that you have to purchase the Mind Valley Program to do CCB. Instead, what I am trying to say is that, like Diego, you can incorporate any positive program into it, including visualization, meditation, or manifesting.

Remember, the objective is to do the opposite of

hammering your brain with stressful thoughts. You must have a clear state of mind for no more than twenty minutes. This is so you can continue with the other Morning Zen steps.

To recap this first block, make sure you have a digital clock and put it in front of your bed where you can see it. Then turn off your cellphone or put it in airplane or do-not-disturb mode until you are ready to go to work.

Next, remember you will need to wake up at least 35 minutes before your regular wake-up time. It's critical that you wake up with no alarm, so you have to program your mind just before you go to sleep by repeating men-tally exactly what time you want to wake up. You can set the alarm just in case, but please do not rely on it. Then go to sleep.

The next day, you won't believe it, but you will wake up near the time you programmed in your head (if not, repeat the technique that night for the next morning).

Forget about your cellphone. Don't even look at the time or any messages at all. As soon as you wake up, de-activate the "just in case" alarm.

Go to the kitchen and, on an empty stomach, prepare your Morning Concoction, which can be two fingers of hot water, lime, and a pinch of sodium bicarbonate. Mix it all and voilà.

Once you finish your drink, go back to your room, turn on your device (anything but your cellphone), and put on your meditation program, which could be Deepak Chopra's 21-Day Abundance Challenge (no ads).

Practice all of this for a week (Monday to Friday), and once you've incorporated these three habits into your morning routine, we are ready for the second block.

Congratulations and welcome to Morning Zen. Hit it!

CHAPTER 6

ADAPTATION

Morning Zen

Adrian Gonzalez

Instagram: @the_morning_zen

CHAPTER 6

ADAPTATION

Once you start practicing Morning Zen, you may notice that you will complete it very easily on some days, but you may miss it on others. And guess what? This is understandable. As with any new routine, there will be new steps to follow, new changes to your schedule, and some things will need to be fit in for them to happen flawlessly, so I encourage you to keep practicing.

The important thing is to do it constantly and not lose perseverance in incorporating it into your morning routine, because things are about to get better.

Maybe you are currently practicing other morning

tasks, such as watering your plants, praying, exercising, etc. Well, the magic of Morning Zen is that you can adapt your routines to it, and it will still work.

I had a similar situation. I am a pet lover, and back in the day, one dog breed was very popular in my country: French Bulldogs. The breed enthralled me too, and finally, thanks to my great friend Guillermo Oscar, I got one. Her name is Dakota.

She is a dark brindle with a white chest, cute as hell, and always by my side. Her favorite dish is salmon, and she can turn into a little beast if another dog touches her food. To sum up, she is cute but psycho.

When Dakota was a little puppy, I had to teach her to do her necessities outside. But little puppies have little bladders and cannot go for long without peeing. As a matter of fact, there is a rule that says puppies can hold their pee for a number of hours equal to their age in months. For example, if your puppy is six months old, it can only hold its pee for six hours, which means that you have to take it out several times a day or have a dog pad nearby, ready for their accidents. Because of this, one of the first things in the morning that I have to do is take Dakota out for her morning walk.

You might be asking, "What did you do with Morning

Zen?" Well, interestingly, I adapted it, making it a little parenthesis in my routine. Now I wake up with no alarm, brush my teeth, prepare my morning concoction, and take Dakota out. Then, when I come back, without grabbing my cellphone at all, I continue my Morning Zen as usual.

So, feel free to adapt your Morning Zen practice. If you need to perform a significant task, do it beforehand, incorporate it into the practice, or, as recommended, do it after Morning Zen ends.

Some of you might now be saying, "Adrian, I am married with children. My current routine is already difficult to complete, and now, with the Morning Zen, I don't know if I can make it." Well, guess what, it can be done. Morning Zen is that adaptable. People going through a divorce or with children have made it fit into their mornings. Indeed, people often include their family in the Morning Zen routine, and it has worked out extraordinarily. As the famous American film critic Pauline Kael once said, "Where there's a will, there's a way."

Author James Clear explains in his book *Atomic Habits* that to build new habits, you need to follow four rules that train our brain to crave the new behavior and stick with it over the long term: make it obvious, make it attractive, make it easy, and make it satisfying.

Make it obvious. Check! Why is Morning Zen obvious? Because most of its habits are popular, all of them have positive outcomes, and you can practice them as part of your daily routine, making it simple to do them without setting an expectation to accomplish. With Morning Zen, great habits lead to positive results. Just follow the steps, and as a result, it becomes obvious that you should do them.

Make it attractive. Morning Zen is amazingly attractive because, without noticing and just following the steps in this book, you will complete more than ten good habits every day.

Make it easy. As I explained before, this routine can be done anywhere. You don't need equipment, other people, or a special place to do it. And the steps are easy to perform. Remember, no sweat or pain is included.

Make it satisfying. One thing about Morning Zen is that you will feel great just a few days after starting to practice it. And you will begin to notice results and satisfaction in your way of life. Believe me, you will experience rewards almost as soon as you start doing the complete Morning Zen routine. You won't believe it at first, but you will as soon you start practicing every day.

Morning Zen is adaptable to your schedule, and once you realize that you can have an amazing morning every day, it becomes effortless to do it. It is easy, attractive, and satisfying, and best of all, no major physical effort is involved.

Knowing this, we are now ready to jump into the next chapter, where I share part of my journey on pursuing happiness, which I am sure you will like.

CHAPTER 7

PURSUIT

OF HAPPINESS

Morning Zen

Adrian Gonzalez

Instagram: @the_morning_zen

CHAPTER 7

PURSUIT OF HAPPINESS

There was a period when I was focused on searching deeply for a way to be happier in my daily life. I did a lot of research and interviews, read books, watched documentaries, and studied anything that I could get my hands on so I could develop a formula and, as a result, level up my happy state of mind.

I will very quickly summarize what I discovered. First, there are two types of happiness: extrinsic and intrinsic. Extrinsic happiness, which comes from the Latin root *extrinsecus*, meaning "on the outside," comes from external situations, events, or experiences, like image, money, possessions, and status. Things that can lead to extrinsic happiness include a new car, a new house, vacations, a raise, a new position in the company, and, why not, winning the lottery. All that comes from external events and material things.

On the other hand, there is intrinsic happiness, which comes from the things we do, such as sharing, helping, and growing. As its Latin root, *intrinsecus*, suggests, intrinsic happiness comes from inside us. It's like when you were a little kid and you did a simple task in your home because, naturally, you wanted to make your mom or dad happier. For example, when I was a little kid, I enjoyed making breakfast for my mom on Sundays and carrying it to her bed as a surprise. I recall that I was happy doing all of this because I wanted to share and spoil my mom so she could be happy, and my mom's happiness and satisfaction automatically made me happier. This is how intrinsic happiness works.

One day, I watched a documentary on Netflix by Roko Belic called *Happy*. This documentary, released in 2011, interviewed people who could be considered incredibly happy. They were of different ages, genders, income levels, and cultures, and they came from different parts of the world.

One person caught my attention, a guy from the

corporate world. If I am not mistaken, he was a computer manager in a bank, and he was eager to become the youngest bank director. In the interview, he confessed that this bank spoiled him with a good income and, as a result, he spent a lot of money on stuff like fashion. He enjoyed it, and in general, he had a good life.

Well, one day, this guy was invited to help as a volunteer in a hospice for the sick, destitute, and dying, established by St. Mother Teresa in Kalighat, Kolkata, India. People brought to the home received medical attention and were given the opportunity to die with dignity.

When this guy volunteered, he connected with a dying boy, maybe 15 years old. He helped this teenager by feeding him, and from there, he understood that his vocation was to help these people at that hospice. After that day, he left his job, position, and corporate ladder and dedicated himself to helping people who have been rescued from the streets and needed shelter. In a humble way, he communicated how committed he is to helping these needy people and how happy it makes him.

He finishes the interview with this quote: "You serve your brother in front of you, who is in need, and it gives you a fulfilled, happy life. Perfect, no?" His name is Andy Wimmer.

I have a bachelor's in telecommunications and worked with computers for a while, and from out of the blue, I felt totally connected with Andy's experience. From there, I started to argue with the experience. I wanted to do volunteer work and find this happy feeling that Andy got from helping others.

So, I did some research and reserved a couple of Saturdays to go and visit Hogar Bolivar in Panama City, Panama. Hogar Bolivar is a non-profit organization established in 1883, an asylum dedicated to the elderly. They help, support, and take care of old people who have been abandoned or left with no family for the rest of their days.

Hogar Bolivar receives support through state subsidies, donations, and volunteering. If you would like to do some charity one day, feel free to contact and support them. They do great work for these aged and humble people.

So, in pursuit of this happiness, I offered myself as a volunteer to aid the staff with anything they needed, from helping the elderly go to the bathroom to serving them food and feeding them. I also took the residents for strolls, talked with them, played famous songs that they requested on my acoustic guitar, kept them company, and listened to their life stories—and all of this inside the

Hogar Bolivar facilities.

And wow, I don't know if the experience made me happy, but I can tell you that it was like taking five tequila shots mixed with a glass of vodka combined with a Mike Tyson uppercut to the face that says: "This is how humility tastes; be humble and be grateful." Once in a while, I had to take a break and race to the nun's office, searching for a place where nobody could see me burst into tears.

Now I can tell you that it was a beautiful experience. Surely, it did not make me happier right away, but it made me appreciate many things that come with intrinsic happiness. It made me understand that other things provide us happiness, such as close, connected relationships with our loved ones, family, and friends. Serve. Be empathic, kind to other people, and have the desire to help. If there is a way for you to practice one of these things, or all of them, go ahead and do it. You won't regret it.

If you ask me which happiness is better, well, both give us happiness. If you win the lottery, won't you be happy? And if you help someone and appreciate the satisfaction of that action, won't it make you happy? The answer in both cases is yes. The thing is, as we defined, extrinsic happiness depends on things on the outside, and some of them are out of our control, while intrinsic happiness comes from doing things that we can control and can therefore be repeated and stay longer with us.

But the real issue comes from human behavior, which makes us feel and compare the happiness that we are living and our normal state of mind. This is what psychologists called the hedonic treadmill, or hedonic adaptation, and it is the process by which the affective impact of emotions or events is reduced over time.

The term "hedonic treadmill" was coined by Brickman and Campbell in their article "Hedonic Relativism and Planning the Good Society" (1971), which describes the tendency of people to keep a fairly stable baseline level of happiness despite external events and fluctuations in demographic circumstances. The process of hedonic adaptation is often conceptualized as a treadmill since, no matter how hard one tries to gain an increase in happiness, one will remain in the same place.

But this behavior has a bright side, and it is the magic of our mind. As with most adaptations, it serves to protect and enhance our perception of things over time. Therefore, when there are people who have gone through an unfortunate event, and their lives have dramatically changed, when asked if they have experienced happy moments in their new situation, often answer yes. This means that our mind can adapt to new situations and environments and reset the mood and state of humor we feel, giving us the capacity to feel the same happiness we experienced years before.

This is why, when a romantic relationship ends, after a prudent time, you can feel happy again. Our mind automatically reacts to the new situation and says, "Ok, months have passed. We've set the happy levels back on track, and we are ready to experience and enjoy happy moments again."

And that is magic. This explains the famous phrase: "Time heals all." But the true meaning should be: "Do not worry. We have hedonic adaptation, and after a prudent time, you will adapt, you will feel better, and your mind will be ready to experiment and appreciate happy moments again." So, if you are reading this book and passing through a difficult situation, please rely on this behavior, and after a time, you will enjoy the sensation of feeling happy moments again.

The issue comes when we don't want to accept this new situation and we fight with hedonic adaptation, making it harder to progress and heal. That is why, when things happen, the first thing psychologist recommend is to accept them. That sends a message to our brain to deal with them, thus beginning hedonic adaptation and the internal overcoming of this experience.

On the other hand, the hedonic treadmill also has a downside. When we are happy because something positive arrives in our life, we enjoy it, but after a time, the hedonic treadmill begins to work, and this new thing becomes the standard until we adapt to it, and we stop feeling the same level of happiness that we used to. That is why, when we get a raise, at first, we are very happy with it. We enjoy it, but with time, we start to feel the same way we did before.

But guess what? There is a way that we can fight back against the hedonic treadmill, or at least delay it, so we can continue to enjoy the happy moments in our lives.

And what is that secret? The answer is simple. **Be grateful**. But when I ask people about this, they nod at me and tell me that they are grateful, and then they explain to me that it is more mental than anything else. Meaning, they are grateful when they are praying or because of something good just happened, or by appreciating the good things in life. Or they might say, "Thank you," as a polite way of responding to something that has been given to them. But the main concept is that they do not perform the practice of gratitude as a regular habit in their life.

Hence, in this chapter, I will help you incorporate the habit of being grateful and, why not, having a happier life because of Morning Zen.

After you finish Collected Conscious Breathing, you will take a blank sheet of paper, letter size (8.5" x 11"), and divide it into three rectangles that are roughly the same size. If you would like me to be more detailed about this, I will tell you that I am not the New Kids on the Block, but here is the step-by-step.

Take the sheet of paper and turn it horizontally. Divide it into three vertical rectangles of the same size, and then tear the sheet into three columns. Now you have three small sheets of paper of the same size. We will work with one column per day, so take one and put the rest away for now. Next, with the column in the vertical position, divide it into upper and lower parts. In fact, you can also draw a line across the middle to make this division clearer for your eyes.

In the upper part, start writing in any order three things that you are thankful for. Put them as bullets; no need for numbers. At first, it might be tough to think of what you should write there, but as I explained, we need to delay the hedonic treadmill when it comes to the great things that we have or the awesome things that have happened to us by listing them on paper.

By this, I mean being grateful for those things we have now that we didn't have before. It could be the better salary that you are already earning or a new laptop or cellphone. It could be anything. In fact, you can even be thankful for the AC unit in your room that is working while you are reading this book.

Remember, you may have nice things on hand today, and it may already seem normal for you to have them, but certainly, in this world, someone would kill to have them but does not, and for that, you should be grateful.

You may be asking, "Adrian, why should it be handwritten? Why not write them on a laptop or an electronic device?" Well, let me tell you that, as a techy guy, without a doubt, I tried it, but something is lacking when you do this. Let me explain further.

We have been hardwired since childhood to handwrite things, as a tool for taking notes, to communicate with others, and as a way to learn and understand things in life. So, when you handwrite something, it makes a better connection with your mind. This is how we have been designed. In one way, handwriting enhances our memory because we unconsciously repeat that word or sentence in our mind to write it.

Typing on a keyboard does not do the same because it is a more mechanical way to write. Pressing a key or the device's display skips the process of drawing the letters that help to connect better with our brain. To put it another way, your hands become an extension of your brain when you draw the letter of a word, phrase, or sentence.

For example, imagine you are the director of a symphony orchestra, or as in German, the Kapellmeister, and you have to practice a masterpiece in your mind to feel the sensation of connecting with that musical piece. And let's say that you have two tools to do this, but neither uses sound.

One is the conductor's baton, which is the stick that the directors use to communicate to the orchestra the pace, tempo, cues, or character of the music they are playing.

The other tool is a piano keyboard with no sound, but you can practice the cords and melody of the music while connecting with it. Using both tools, you will need to repeat the song or melody in your brain, or you can even hum it while you play it in your head.

Let's say that, first, you will use the director's baton. If you use the stick, unconsciously you will be more connected because, in a way, you will be using an extension of your body to express the tempo and melody of the piece. You are kind of drawing the song's pace with the stick, and as a result, you will feel more connected while humming the song in your mind.

Now, let's say you use the second tool, the piano keyboard with no sound. You will also hum the melody while pressing keys, but this process comes in a mechanical way. And of course, you can imagine in your head how the melody will sound, and from the force of pressing the keys, you can reflect on the volume or intensity of the melody, but unfortunately, the sensation may not be the same.

By this, I'm not saying that a professional pianist cannot sense the greatness of a masterpiece just by mimicking playing the piano. I'm saying that using our arms and hands to interpret a song will form a better connection with our body and, therefore, our mind.

It's like dancing while humming a song versus mimic being a DJ while humming a song. Which of these will make you feel more connected to the song?

So, writing by hand on a sheet of paper is a better way to express gratitude, meaning it's a better way to delay the hedonic treadmill in your brain. Thus, my recommendation is to lean on handwriting.

So, what are the other benefits of practicing the habit of gratitude? Well, being grateful makes us better appreciate all the things we have in our life. We practice being humbler, and this generates awareness of all the blessings that we have been given during the ride of our life.

Furthermore, we should be grateful for those things in our life that occurred but that we might not have wanted to.

For example, let's say that you are passing through a difficult moment in your life. Generally, there are two ways to see this situation. One is to blame, complain, or struggle with how or why it happened until it gets resolved. The other is to accept it and be grateful for the experience.

This second option is usually the hardest to follow, but when you do, you will certainly learn from the experience, grow from it, and become a savvier person. So, remember to also be grateful for the results you weren't expecting; they may provide you with lessons that you will someday use.

For example, when a friend of mine was getting a divorce—and with a daughter to worry about, too—I suggested that it was an excellent opportunity for him to practice during Morning Zen the habit of gratitude for what he was going through, meaning, being thankful for the divorce process that he was experiencing. At first, he declined, and he asked me how and why. So, I explained to him that he could have two attitudes in this difficult process.

One was that the separation could be the hell he expected it to be, and the other was that he could realize that separating came with a gift, therefore, he should enjoy the process. And if this process came with appreciating other things, he should be thankful for that.

So, as the days passed, he started to write down on his sheets of paper his thanks for the separation process he was going through, and with this, he began a process of forgiveness.

This gave him a new perspective on the situation, and as a result, the experience turned into a painless process, and he happily overcame that difficult situation.

Today he has a wonderful relationship with his ex-wife, and he still thanks me for that.

So, if you are passing through a difficult moment, accept it and start being grateful for it so you can forgive, learn, and grow because of it. By doing this, you are deciding to be happier.

And in case you are asking if these three lines of thankfulness have to be the same every day, the answer is no. I recommend you vary them and write down what you truly feel grateful for during Morning Zen.

Gratitude is the first habit of the second block of Morning Zen.

If you'd like to read a funny basketball story, you should continue to the next chapter; you will love it. But to resume this chapter, take this new sheet of paper, draw a line down the middle, and, in the upper part, write three things that you are grateful for.

Write them cleanly and elegantly. Make an effort, like it might be read by another person in the room. Now, don't worry—this is your personal paper, so what you write should not be read by anyone but yourself—but try to write the lines with calmness, kindness, and your best handwriting. Enjoy it and do it with love.

Once you've finished these three lines of gratitude, you are ready for the next habit of Morning Zen.

To close this chapter, I would like to share this great phrase from Gaur Gopal Das, a Hindi motivational speaker, in which he explains why gratitude is a key part of happiness: "We are so busy trying to get what we like that we forget to like what we get."

CHAPTER 8

YOU CAN CALL IT

A MIRACLE

Morning Zen

Adrian Gonzalez

Instagram: @the_morning_zen

CHAPTER 8

YOU CAN CALL IT A MIRACLE

"Darling, I had the best intentions, but I dug myself a hole with a modern invention." – The Submarines

Let me begin this chapter by telling you a story from when I was a little kid. Back in the day, in my neighborhood, there was a basketball court built so all the kids from the block could learn and practice this amazing sport. We also had a well-loved coach, Fermín Octavio "Tavo" Castañeda, also known as "Prof Tavo" or just "Prof," which is short for "professor." In the summer, he and his team ran the famous Mini Basketball League, also known as "La Mini," which consisted of a little tournament of four teams distinguished by color: the Reds,

111

Yellows, Blues, Greens. It was called the Mini Basketball League because it was for kids between the ages of three and thirteen. I do not know if it was a lucky charm, but most of the time, the Green team won the tournament, while the Yellow team usually finished last.

Then, how were these teams formed? In the first two weeks of summer, Coach Tavo held practices and tryouts, and from there, he began to identify which player fit better with what team. When I was seven, I wanted to be on the Green team no matter what. During the scouting for the teams, I remember repeating to myself several times a day, "I want to be on the Green Team. I want to be on the Green team. I want to be on the Green team".

After the two weeks of practices and tryouts, the day came for Coach Tavo to select the teams. Before the selection, the kids were seated in a circle in the middle of the court, waiting to be picked, and Coach Tavo assigned them according to size, age, skills, and abilities. I remember that he took his time with this selection because he wanted all the teams to be as balanced as possible. He called kids one by one, directing them to the corner for the team they would be on for the summer.

When it was my turn, I took a deep breath, and he assigned me to a team of players I identified with. Then he did the same with the rest of the kids until all the teams were formed.

The next stage, color assignation, was similar to a little raffle.

The captains of each team had to choose one of four folded slips of paper, each of which had the name of a color written on it: red, yellow, green, and blue. Obviously, the selection was random because no one could see which color was written on each slip of paper.

When it was our turn, our captain randomly chose one of the four slips of paper, and when he unfolded it, like magic, it said: "Green." And from that day forward, I noticed that if I pronounce a wish or intention continuously for several days, from out of the blue, it will occur. At the time, I thought this was interesting, and as a result, I was very happy. But the story does not end there.

The next week, the uniforms arrived. They were delivered at a specific date and time, and they were handed out in a FIFO process; this means first in, first out. What often happened was that, for X or Y reason, a couple of kids could not make it to team selections. However, they could come the day the uniforms arrived, and at that time, they would be assigned to a team that had spare uniforms. This meant that if you missed the day when the uniforms

113

were delivered, then another kid might get your uniform instead. Worst-case scenario, you could play but with another t-shirt of the same color.

It sounds like a miscalculation, but on the bright side, there was a kind of workaround: it did not matter if a team ran out of uniforms; the important part was that all the kids could play in the Mini League. Additionally, as everything in life has a cost, to get a uniform, you had to pay for it, meaning they were not free.

On uniform delivery day, I was running an errand with my grandmother, and I totally forgot. When we got back home, the delivery time had passed, and to top it all off, near my house, there was a neighbor with his uniform on, who said, "I am ready to play in the Mini Basket League."

I immediately started to stress and ran out to my grandma, Mercedes Rodriguez, and told her, "Abuela Merce, I missed the schedule for the uniform delivery." Suddenly, because of my impotence at that moment, my eyes filled with tears.

My Grandma said, "Hey, little kid, no worries. You have to stay positive. You will get your uniform. They are waiting for you."

I explained that there was a big chance that my t-shirt had been given to another kid who had missed the team selection day and my team might run out of uniforms. Upon saying those words, I nearly burst into tears. Moreover, my mom was still at work, and I needed the money for the uniform.

When I told my grandma that, she went and got her purse, and then she asked me, "How much is the uniform?" She gave me the exact amount of cash and told me to go for it. However, I was blocked in my head. I already knew that it was too late and I had missed my chance to play in uniform with "Los Verdes."

My grandma saw how upset I was, and she said to me firmly, "Repeat after me. I will get my Green t-shirt uniform. I will get my Green t-shirt uniform..." She made me repeat it several times. Then she told me, "Now, don't stop repeating it, and go to your coach or the organization and ask for your uniform."

With nothing else to lose, I did just that. I remember that with each step I took, I repeated what my grandma had said to me: "I will get my Green t-shirt uniform."

To sum up, 20 minutes later, I returned to my house, went to my grandma, and shouted, "Abuela, I got it! Yes, I have my Green t-shirt uniform, and I will be able to play for the Green team."

My grandma said to me, "See, when you have the intention, you repeat it several times in your head, and you have a positive attitude about it, from out of nowhere, it will happen."

Since then, I have understood that intentions exist.

That season, I began to understand what it is to feel love for your favorite sport, which for me was basketball. Even better, that year, my team, the Green team, won the championship. Maybe you can call it luck. I call it intention.

As a kid, I understood that intentions work, but guess what? With the passing of time and me growing up, I forgot to practice what my grandma had taught me.

Have you ever had a similar situation? Have you been positive about something and repeated to yourself what you want to happen, and then, from out of nowhere, it happens? Well, that is called intention, and it exists.

There are many documentaries and books about intention, like *The Secret* by Rhonda Byrne. An American writer and famous motivational speaker named Dr. Wayne Dyer, who dedicated his life to investigating and promoting the power of positive attitudes and successful mindsets. One of his last books was called *The Power of Intention*. In it, he defines intention as a force in the universe that allows the act of creation to take place. Therefore, intention is not something you do, but energy you are a part of.

During my continuous learning path in life, I signed up for a seminar delivered by Ismael Cala. He is a Cuban journalist, former CNN Español reporter, writer, and motivational speaker for the region. In the seminar, "Maestría de Vida," meaning "Life Mastery" (if you have the opportunity, sign up for it; he teaches a lot of interesting things to apply in life), he taught us about the three things he practices in the morning that were excellent for his daily journey: mindfulness, gratefulness, and intention. I was already doing the first two as part of my daily routine, but the third one, intention, I found interesting, and I incorporated it into my Morning Zen.

A lot of people call intention the universe, the favorable result of coincidences, or energy. Call it what you will, but if you ask me, "Adrian, does intention work?" The answer is YES, it does.

And during this journey what I learned is that intention must be decisive, reachable, and incisive for us to get what we want in life.

Decisive. The intention must be something you want very much, where the desire comes from your guts.

Reachable. Let's say that you have the intention of winning the lottery, but if you do not buy lottery tickets, how do you expect to win it? The intention has to be something you can reach.

Incisive. You have to constantly think about it and be laser focused on the intention you're looking for.

Like me, I am sure that a lot of people believe in intention. Their question is: "Why don't we practice it?" The answer is because we do not perform it as a habit. In Morning Zen, we will incorporate it, and I will tell you how.

Remember the paper where you wrote down your gratitude in the top part? Now we will use the bottom part of that page, and there we will write down three intentions. And those intentions must be written in the present tense, use NLP, and be very specific.

Present: The first word you will start your sentence with is "Today."

NLP: This stands for neuro-linguistic programming and was created by Richard Bandler and John Grinder. They claim that there is a connection between neurological processes (neuro-), language (linguistic), and behavioral patterns learned through experience (programming) and that these can be changed to achieve specific goals in life. For this exercise, it means that you are not going to write the intention as though it will happen in the future. Instead, you will write it as though you are sure that it will start at any moment during the day. In other words, avoid using the verb "will" and instead use "going to."

Specific. You must describe in as much detail as possible the exact thing you want. This means, if your intention is to have a new car, you cannot just write "new car." Instead, you need to describe it, meaning you need to write down the type of car, brand, model, year, and even color. For example: "Today I am going to find a car dealer, and he is going to sell me a brand-new, four-door red Mini Cooper Countryman SUV that is in my budget."

Now I will give you the format of these intentions and how to write them down.

Just as you wrote three lines about your gratitude, you will also write three lines for your intentions. The difference is that these intentions have to attack different terms of your life. Now let me explain how:

The first line will be your middle or long-term intentions. For example, you want to buy a new house, but you know that you don't have the money right now. However, you are sure that you will complete the down payment in a couple of months, or it's in your middle-term plans.

The second line should be the intention of the day. For instance, it could be a deal you want to close, a thing you want to get resolved, or that nice thing you want to happen to you.

As for the third line, "you can call it a miracle." And in case you don't believe in miracles, I can tell you that when you begin to write them down in your intentions, you will start to.

So, you will make an exception for this third line, and you won't be specific with what you write. As a matter of fact, you will just write down the following: "Today a miracle is going to happen to me."

John Lennon once said, "Life is what happens to you while you're busy making other plans." Well, I have a similar phrase that I want to share with you: "Miracles are what happen while you are busy doing something else."

From now on, you will start to notice that miracles are happening in your life. You will feel more blessed, and as a result, you will start to appreciate new peaks of happiness in your life.

Write these three lines on the paper in the format suggested, and soon you will start to notice the power of intention.

One fact about intention is that we should not stick to the results. Or, as Deepak Chopra better explained it: we should pay attention to the present, have intention for the future, and be detached from the results. This means that we should promote our intentions, but sometimes we have to let the universe do its work. That could take time, so we definitely have to detach or get rid of anxiety about the results we want for that specific intention.

There is a free Chopra meditation that talks about the laws of intention and detachment, and in it, he provides the following great example.

Imagine a situation where you are speaking about some specific topic and you forget the name of a person you want to mention. So, what do you do? You start thinking and rethinking about that name, meaning you have instant intention to recall it but cannot. Then you have to release or detach yourself from that action because you have to continue the conversation.

But suddenly, after time passes, from out of the blue, the name of the person you were trying to recall flashes into your mind. And you remember it crystal clear.

Well, a similar process works with our intentions. We need to understand that we have to write them down and detach from the results. If it is for you, it will occur on its own.

Intention is the second habit of the second block of Morning Zen.

So, to sum up, take the sheet of paper on which you wrote your three lines of gratitude and in the lower half, write your three intentions: the middle or long-term intention, the daily intention, and the miracle.

Again, make sure to use your best handwriting.

Now you are ready for the next step, what to do with that paper, so get ready and follow me to the next chapter.

CHAPTER 9

LET THE UNIVERSE

DO THE WORK

Morning Zen

Adrian Gonzalez

Instagram: @the_morning_zen

CHAPTER 9

LET THE UNIVERSE DO THE WORK

As I mentioned before, you can put any name you want on where the blessing of an answered intention comes from. You can call it the universe, God, energy, any name you prefer and feel comfortable with, or the one that gives you the conviction that it works. And with this, I will explain the next step to follow. In addition, the next chapter is one of my favorites to practice in Morning Zen, so I recommend that after you finish this one, which is very short, you immediately jump to the next one.

You may be asking, "What do we do with these sheets of paper with our gratitude statements and our intentions?" Well, it's simple. The next step is to reread everything you wrote, starting at the top. Try to read the lines aloud, confirming all the things that you wrote. Once you finish, you will fold the paper twice and deliver it to the universe.

And how do you do that? Easy. Just tear the sheet of paper into smaller pieces and throw them into the near-est wastebasket in your room or bathroom. By doing this, you are telling the universe that you have confirmed what you are grateful for, and your intentions are ready to happen. And because you have read the paper, folded, torn, and tossed away, you are now ready to receive the outcome from it.

Maybe you are asking, "Why throw away our inten-tions?" No worries. In fact, you are doing the opposite, telling the universe that you have accomplished your part and closed the window and now it's time for the uni-verse, God, or the universal energy to do its part. That is why, instead of using an entire sheet of paper, we only use a piece of it, so we can be more efficient in this pro-cess and take care of our planet just a little more.

Now that you are waking up with no alarm, drinking your Morning Concoction, meditating, writing down what you are grateful for and your intentions, and send-ing them to the universe, you are ready to boost your morning with the next step.

Meanwhile, it's okay for you to begin practicing gratitude and intention as soon as tomorrow. As I mentioned before, this book is designed for you to practice Morning Zen in parallel with your reading, so go ahead and incorporate the steps. Don't wait to finish the book to start doing Morning Zen. Enjoy it and feel free to start as soon as you can.

CHAPTER 10

THE POWER OF MUSIC

Morning Zen

Adrian Gonzalez

Instagram: @the_morning_zen

CHAPTER 10

THE POWER OF MUSIC

"Music is life itself." –Louis Armstrong

As I'm convinced that you have already experienced, music is a fundamental part of our existence. We listen to music as kids, and from there, it accompanies us for the rest of our lives.

But the difference in Morning Zen is that we are going to develop the practice of listening to good music. Now, you may be asking, "Adrian, what do you mean by good music?" For me, it's not about specific rhythms, BPM (beats per minute), artists, or genre. Instead, I define it as Happy Healthy Music. Later I will explain in detail why

I use this name.

Before continuing with this chapter, we must verify first that you have speakers, because they are an important tool for this new habit. If you don't have them in your room, I suggest you go and get some, preferably a portable Bluetooth speaker so you can move it around as needed.

Now, let's get back on track. For some decades now, scientists and psychologists have found that music can improve our mood and productivity. For example, have you heard about the famous Mozart effect? Well, a study was done in which Mozart's music was played for a group of people to see if it improved task performance, and the results showed an improvement in cognitive abilities.

Other studies have shown that any kind of music the listener enjoys will provide the same results. This means that music has a positive influence on us.

In everyday life, it's easy to see the leverage that music has over everything else. It can be found in movies, video games, stores, etc. For example, it has been shown that electronic dance music creates an urgency to buy. Going deeper, have you ever been in a Zara store? If you haven't noticed, they have several nice playlists of EDM music for when you are trying on or buying clothes. The music gives you the sensation that you are enjoying what you are wearing, and sometimes it can transport you in your mind to where you can use a particular clothes combination that you are about to buy. And believe me, this is not random music that they play. The music played by all the stores must be downloaded from the internal music library at their headquarters.

Nowadays, those playlists are so well-liked that you can search for them on Spotify, YouTube, Soundcloud, or other popular music platforms.

And what about in restaurants? If you ask me, my favorite is the playlist they use in TGI Friday restaurants. They put on such good music that you can go there by yourself to enjoy the playlist as you appreciate a great dish.

So, the next time you get the opportunity to visit one of these places, check out what I'm saying, and you will understand what I mean by the power of music.

I am so passionate about music because it has been in my life for as long as I can remember. As a matter of fact, when I was a baby, I preferred to watch MTV for hours, entranced by all the videos and music they were showing, rather than cartoons. And the MTV I'm talking about is the MTV of the 80's, when they put on nothing but music videos 24/7.

Since then, I've learned to play several instruments, like the clarinet, trumpet, guitar, and drums. I've played in bands and gotten some gigs, so some people call me a musician. However, I prefer to be considered a music lover, as it acknowledges the importance music has in my life.

And what about playing music while you are getting ready in the morning? It helps us get in the mood and gives us energy within the process. Try to recall the last time you played some music while getting ready.

What did it feel like? Wasn't it great?

After confirming that the music we like can help us with cognitive tasks, boost our mood, and create a better atmosphere, I integrated it into Morning Zen. Why? Because, once we finish CCB, Gratitude, and Intention, our body enters a calm state of mind, a very relaxed, peaceful mood. This is great, but to bring Morning Zen to a crescendo, we should include a radical energy boost, and we will do this with music.

Ergo, your next habit in Morning Zen will be to play Happy Healthy Music to boost your awesome morning attitude.

With this comes a little task you need to do. Because music tastes are so personal, you should create your own wake-up playlist for Morning Zen. Try to include music that you like and that will give you the energy boost to generate swag and vitality in your mornings.

You may be saying, "Adrian, I already have several music playlists. Can I integrate them into Morning Zen?" The answer is no, you will need to create a new one, and the reason why will be described in the next few paragraphs.

So, open your favorite music platform and let's start creating your new personal Wake-Up Morning Zen Playlist. But first, I will give you the four golden rules for making it.

Rule 1: You must only include good music, or as I named it previously, **"Happy Healthy Music."** By this, I mean the songs must not include needy parts in the lyrics, things like, "I miss you," "I want you," "I need you," or "you are the reason." In other words, the lyrics cannot contain any word or action of dependency on someone or something or some unrequited feeling.

Instead, these songs must contain phrases that will encourage your happiness and mood. For example, I fully recommend that you include the famous song by the

135

American artist **Pharrell Williams** called **"Happy."** It is upbeat and catchy, and it has nice lyrics.

Rule 2: When it comes to the chorus or a nice verse in the song, you must sing it. For example, in the song mentioned above, when Pharrell goes into the chorus, you should sing out loud, "Because I'm happyyyyyyyy!" and repeat it as many times as you want.

Rule 3: Generate serotonin and dopamine. Serotonin is the key hormone that stabilizes our mood, feelings of well-being, and happiness, and dopamine is a neurotransmitter that plays a role in how we feel pleasure. And when I say generate serotonin and dopamine, I mean dance! Yes, dance. It doesn't matter if you are not a professional dancer; moving your body to the rhythm of the songs is necessary to start raising your levels of serotonin and dopamine. As a result, you will start transmitting positive emotions throughout your anatomy.

According to an article published by Harvard Medical School and written by science writer Scott Edwards, "Dancing and the Brain," says: "Music stimulates the brain's reward centers, while dance activates its sensory and motor circuits."

It also mentions: "A 2003 study in the New England Journal of Medicine by researchers at the Albert Einstein

College of Medicine discovered that dance can decidedly improve brain health." And "According to the researchers, dancing involves both a mental effort and social interaction and that this type of stimulation helped reduce the risk of dementia."

If follows that while you are shouting, "Because I'm happyyyyy!" please proceed to shake those bones, improve your health, and give yourself a big smile 😊. You deserve it. And as I mentioned before, this is one of my favorite parts of Morning Zen. I think it is because I am a former professional dancer as well, and for me, this break proves that I still have the moves LOL. So, do it, no shame. Enjoy and test yourself by showing that you also have the moves, too. Hit it!

If you can't think of what songs to include besides "Happy," no worries; I've got you covered. If you have the Spotify app or use YouTube, just go to the Instagram account @the_morning_zen, and once you click on the bio link, it will take you to the book's info as well as the icons of each platform containing this amazing "Morning Zen Adrian Antonio Gonzalez Wake-Up List." You will see more than 20 songs in English and Spanish that you can use as a guide while you build your own personal list. And if you would like to share the list with friends, go ahead. Sharing is caring.

Now, why do you need your own list? Because, if you include songs that you like and are more familiar to you, you will definitely feel more fulfillment while singing and dancing along to them.

Also, try to include any old song that complies with Rule 1 and recalls a happy moment in your life. It could be a song that reminds you of a trip, moments with friends, school, etc. By including such songs, for a few seconds, you can at least transport yourself to that happy moment when you enjoyed that song for the first time.

Rule 4: The music volume should be at a reasonable level so it can transmit that energy to you. Once, I had the experience of practicing Morning Zen on a trip, and as a tool, I brought my Bluetooth speakers with me.

When it came time to play Happy Healthy Music, I was afraid to wake my roommate. So, when I hit the play button, I had to turn down the music and put my speakers at a very low volume.

As a result, I could not sense the energy and power of the music like I could when it's playing at a good volume. In other words, I could not practice the habit like I was used to because of the low volume. So, it is preferable that you put your speakers at a good volume, and by this, I'm not talking about a party volume. Instead, the music should only be as loud as you need it to be to sense the music through your body. And if you prefer not to put the volume so high because your neighbor or someone in the next room might wake up, try listening with a good pair of headphones as a workaround.

Listening to Happy Healthy Music is the third habit of the second block of Morning Zen.

To sum up, after you've done Collected Conscious Breathing and written down your gratitude statements and intentions, you will be in a peaceful Zen mood, which is good, but now we need to boost our morning to another stage, and this music will be our best ally.

So, after you finish your intentions, proceed to pump up your speakers, play some Happy Healthy Music, and by the way, sing and dance. You will be creating an amazing ambiance for the next habit in Morning Zen, also known as the First Task to Complete in the Morning.

CHAPTER 11

START YOUR MORNING

WITH ORDER

Morning Zen

Adrian Gonzalez

Instagram: @the_morning_zen

CHAPTER 11

START YOUR MORNING WITH ORDER

"The less the mess, the less you fix." – Adrian Gonzalez

In case you suffer from anxiety like me, I will get straight to the point in this chapter. As the title says, with Morning Zen, you will start your morning with order. Consequently, I would like to start this chapter with this great quote that I constantly repeat to myself: "If I start by completing a minimum task in the morning, I will be able to complete major tasks during the day."

At this point, you may ask, "What is this first task that I need to complete early in the morning to feel empowered and organized?" The answer is simple: **make your**

bed. And you may say, "Checked! Because I have a person who does it for me." This person could be your partner, the cleaning lady, or anyone in charge of doing this task for you, but no. This is something you have to do for yourself because it gives you the empowerment of completing your first task of the morning. It gives you the sense that something was disordered and now you have fixed it.

There are times when we know that we are capable of doing such simple tasks, but we do not do them because we are feeling lazy, running late, too busy, or procrastinating, but with this new task, believe me, you will make sure to prove to yourself that making your bed is your first win of the morning. And you did it. Make it, do it. You are telling the universe that you start your day with order and, therefore, are in control of your day. It is easy, and it could take less than four minutes to do. So, when you think about it, it is not a big deal or a time-consuming task.

On the other hand, if you already do it as part of your morning routine, congratulations. Then all you have to do is integrate the habit into Morning Zen.

My next question is, when exactly do you do it? You may say, "Well, I do it before I leave home." The when is important because it comes with a key to understanding this feeling, and that is to do it **right before you take your shower in the morning**. Why? Because, once you finish your shower and go back to your room, when you return, you will see that your bed is nicely made. This will transmit order to your brain. Plus, you will feel that the room is clean, neat, and ready. The bed usually takes up 60% of the space in a room, so if this is 60% clean and ready, most of your room will already be organized. When you jump from the bathroom to your room to find a made bed, you will experience that awesome feeling of entering a tidy room.

If you see this as a non-attractive task, it is because you are focusing on the process. And this is understandable, but the key to performing a new habit with these characteristics is to focus on the result. This means you should visualize the order, neatness, and tranquility of having a clean bed, and therefore, an ordered room.

Trust me, it will change the mood of your morning. It will give you the sensation that your day has just started, and the world will fear you because you are already making things happen today. And the best part is, when you come back from your work, office, or daily life, return home, and enter your room, you will appreciate a clean and made bed—most importantly, a bed made by you. It gives you the sensation of composure and order and that the bed was waiting for you.

Check it, feel it, try it, argue with the experience, and try to remember this explanation and when to do it. And once you have performed this task in the morning, you will understand what I am trying to transmit with this.

In a famous video, a high-ranking officer gives a speech on the importance of making your bed as the first task in the morning, confirming the value of incorporating it into Morning Zen.

He explains why you should make your bed in such a way that I never get tired of listening to the speech, explaining the whole truth of this task. If you get a chance to see this video, you may notice that he is in the military; therefore, the importance of discipline is rooted in his life.

On May 17, 2014, he gave the speech to the University of Texas at Austin graduating class of 2014, and his name is Admiral William H. McRaven.

He is a retired four-star admiral in the United States Navy who served as the ninth commander of the United States Special Operations Command, and in his speech, he says the following:

> If you want to change the world, start by making your bed. If you make your bed every morning, you will accomplish the first task of the day. It will give you a small sense of pride and will encourage you to do another task and another, and another. And at the end of the day, that one task completed will have turned into many tasks completed. Making your bed will also reinforce the fact that the little things in life matter. If you cannot do the little things right, you will never be able to do the big things right. And if you, by chance, have a miserable day, you will come home to a bed that is made. That you made. And a made bed gives you encouragement that tomorrow will be better.

If you are not such an orderly person, here is an opportunity to improve yourself with the help of Morning Zen. By doing this, without noticing it, you are inculcating the habit of creating order in your life.

Now, if you are thinking, "Adrian, my partner is still in bed while I'm starting the Morning Zen, making me unable to perform this first task of the day," well, I suggest the following two options:

1) Try to integrate your partner into your Morning Zen so the habits and good mood can work for both of you. I did with my partner, and as a result, we make the bed together. This means it takes us less time to complete this task, and at the same time, it gives us the sense that we are working as a team. Try this and argue with experience.

2) As a workaround, put the rest of the room in order. This will give you the sensation of a neat room to complement the task of making the bed once you are able to do so. You can also share and assign tasks with your partner. For example, you can agree to put things away, while your partner can make the bed once they wake up. Remember that the objective of this habit is to make you perform a little task in the morning and start your day with order.

Making your bed is the fourth habit of the second block of Morning Zen.

To sum up, wake up with no alarm, turn off your backup alarm, take your Morning Concoction, meditate, write down your gratitude, set your intentions, enhance your mood by playing Happy Healthy Music, and then, accompanied by the great ambiance of the music, make your bed, move, dance, and smile. Then, with all the flow that automatically spreads from you, you will be ready for the next chapter, "The Review of Your Day."

CHAPTER 12

THE REVIEW OF

YOUR DAY

Morning Zen

Adrian Gonzalez

Instagram: @the_morning_zen

CHAPTER 12

THE REVIEW OF YOUR DAY

"I'm so sorry, I totally forget of our meeting today."

"Have you heard about Morning Zen? They've got a habit for that"

—Adrian Gonzalez

One of the advantages that come with the practice of Morning Zen is that, by doing it, you will incorporate the habit of reviewing your day before leaving your place.

This habit comes with two actions. but first, let's go back in history and look at what the mornings of the biggest conquers and commanders who ever existed were like.

Genghis Khan was the founder of the Mongol Empire and is considered the biggest land conqueror in history. Some people refer to him as genocidal, but on the other hand, he had good points. He was in favor of the fair treatment of different ethnic groups, he accepted various religions inside his empire, and he made the Silk Road secure. During his time, they said that you could travel the whole route with a piece of gold on top of your head and never get assaulted. The Silk Road was an ancient trade route linking China with the West, and it carried goods and ideas between the two great civilizations of Rome and China.

His famous technique was the arrow storm, a rain of arrows practiced by Mongols, where he surrounded his enemy and then shot a hail of arrows in such numbers that they seemed a force of nature. And he coined the great phrase: "There is no value in anything until it is finished." In other words, "Almost doesn't count."

Napoleon Bonaparte was a famous left-handed French military and political leader who rose to prominence during the French Revolution and led several successful campaigns during the Revolutionary Wars. He is quoted as saying, "Never interrupt your enemy when he is making a mistake," and "A leader is a dealer in hope."

And what about Alexander the Great? He was the ruler of the ancient Greek kingdom of Macedon. He constructed a massive empire that stretched from Macedonia to Egypt and from Greece to part of India. Alex understood how to build a loyal empire that would aid him in conquering the world. He demonstrated his impressive leadership skills at the forefront of battles, showing characteristics of courage and bravery. His famous phrases, which I have always related to the entrepreneurial spirit, are: "There is nothing impossible to him who will try," and "Each moment free from fear makes a man immortal."

These three emperors have something in common. First, they had a vision of what they wanted to do and were always in pursuit of the next conquest. Second, once they woke up, they would start their morning by reviewing the plan of the day. They did not improvise. They had a plan, and they followed it. This second characteristic is the one that I want to talk about.

If you want to be a visionary or efficient person, you must integrate the great habit of reviewing your day before it starts. By this, I mean you must check your agenda before your workday begins. Why? Because doing this brings three benefits that you will immediately start to notice.

First, you will keep your meetings at the front of your mind. This means there will be no "Oops, I totally forgot about that meeting" because you will have refreshed your memory about it that morning.

Second, you will have a full view of what is going to be your day, and with this, you will organize yourself better, rearranging things when needed, and if there is any urgency or change of plans, you will certainly manage the situation better.

Third, it will give you a sense of how your day will be, so you will be more conscious and prepared for it. For example, let's say you're a professional boxer and you will have a fight soon, but you don't review who your opponent will be. Boxing with an opponent selected by random choice is much different than boxing with the world champion. As soon as you think about it, you will have a different mindset, and your day will flow from that.

Maybe you are one of those structured people who do a similar review before going to bed. This can lead to you unconsciously bringing the stress of the next day to your sleep; consequently, there's a big chance that you will be unable to sleep well. But if you have the confidence that you have a process for the next morning where you will have time to check your schedule before your day starts, then you may have the best of both worlds: sleeping without thinking of the future and checking your agenda before your workday begins.

Remember that every day is like a battle, and do you think that the great conquerors above just went to battle as soon as they woke up? Certainly not. They already had a plan, and they would check it and the status of their troops, and then, they would give the orders for the day.

This is similar to what happens every morning of our lives. We shouldn't start our day by waking up and then immediately resolving issues, making decisions within seconds of a problem arriving, and becoming a "fire-fighter."

We shouldn't wake up, grab our phones, and start replying to messages first thing in the morning.

You need to be on top of how your day will be. That is one of the objectives of Morning Zen. You should be in control of your mornings rather than the mornings in control of you, so as part of what you learned to do this chapter, you will start performing the habit of checking your agenda/calendar by quickly looking over your schedule. This will give you a full view of your day.

Remember that things will happen during the day that will be out of your control, but reviewing your day and formulating a plan of action will let you know how your day will be so you can effectively battle and conquer it.

And what about knowing what to wear for the day? Well, with this habit you will be killing two birds in one stone, meaning you will review your day by swiftly checking your meetings and, with that in mind, proceed to put on clothes for the occasion.

Let's say you are a salesperson or a business developer or, because of the nature of your job, you have to be in meetings with people inside or outside your organization. In that case, how you look, meaning what you are wearing, is very important. It takes less than four seconds for our minds to judge someone based on their looks, so it is important to always look good. Or, as an urban way to say it, you should look "fresh to death."

On the other hand, let's say that you are one of those people who are very practical, meaning you always wear similar clothes. In that case, the habit of checking your agenda before the day starts will always be a final double-check of your attire. For example, no matter what clothes I'm wearing, I always like to put on sneakers because of their comfort and style, but for some meetings, it's important to wear the proper attire, meaning I cannot attend in sneakers but have to wear appropriate shoes.

And in case you must wear a uniform every day, then it's better because you save those minutes in the morning of thinking what to wear. Therefore, you can focus on checking who you are going to meet and how your day will be.

If you are a person who likes to take your time when selecting the clothes, you are going to wear the next day and that is why you prefer to do it the night before, well, that's understandable. Just remember that recalling a meeting days before is not the same as remembering it the same day, so I recommend doing this double-check each morning.

Now, you may be saying, "Okay, Adrian, you've sold me on the concept, and it sounds like an interesting habit to practice. Now, how should I apply it in Morning Zen?" Well, the answer is more like **review to know and check to dress**.

This means, once you get out of the shower, with your Happy Healthy Music on in the background and before you start getting ready, open your agenda, calendar, or day schedule. Check to see if you have any meetings and if you have to dress a specific way.

The best thing about this habit is that you are telling the universe that you are set and dressed for your work-day before your nine-to-five begins. Therefore, you are "locked and loaded" and prepared for the day.

This process is really quick and effective, and it should not take you more than 45 seconds to check your agenda.

And if you are thinking, "Well, Adrian, I have my agenda on my cellphone," this is a red flag. Well, I can understand, and this is important to explain. Morning Zen is a cellphone detox timeframe in your mornings, so if you have your agenda or calendar on your cellphone, you have to be very conscious about what you are doing when you grab it. This means you need to forget about anything that may pop up on your notification screen or any message that may call your attention. You must think about one and only one thing: checking your agenda without any other distraction. So, prepare yourself men-tally and then go ahead and pull up your calendar or schedule app, check your agenda, and review your day.

It is mandatory that you focus only on checking your agenda and hold the cellphone no longer than 45 seconds so you don't get immersed in the other things on it that are waiting for you to check them.

Remember, avoid being a firefighter. Instead, review your day and check with whom you will meet and the subject of your meetings. That will give you the landscape of how your day will be and the mindset of what to expect from it, making you readier for your daily battle.

Maybe you are asking, "Adrian, my agenda is not as full of meetings because of the nature of my job or my day." In that case, I suggest using your schedule as a Timebox, or Timeboxing. And what do I mean by Timeboxing? It is a practice that many productive people use, and well, I define it as the art of putting your to-do list tasks into time frames inside your agenda during your week.

Most of us create a list of pending things that are a must to complete, and for these, we create the famous to-do list. From it, we know we have these pending tasks to complete, but sometimes we are unable to do them all because other things need to be resolved or we were unable to find the time to do them. So, for these, the best practice is to assign each to-do task a timeframe inside your schedule or agenda.

Don't get me wrong. I am not saying that the to-do list is not important. In fact, I have a to-do list, but it's for making sure I separate the time in my calendar to complete those tasks. Try doing this, and you will see that you will be more productive. Now I will give you four tips for programming your Timebox:

1) Set real and worst-case-scenario time. This means that if you have an activity that can take you from 30 to 45 minutes, then allocate 45 minutes in the agenda. When the time comes, compete with yourself by setting in your mind 30 minutes as a goal. Once you start the activity, say to yourself, "I have these 30 minutes to finish," and you will put pressure on yourself to do it faster. By this, I do not mean that you have to be in a rush to complete your task; instead, you are saying to yourself, "Be focused, sharp, and on time." Having this type of self-obligation will make you get better at finishing your daily tasks because, unconsciously, you will be reducing the time needed to complete them.

Let's say that you ought to reply to an email to your boss or teammate with an update list. Because it's something that you need to focus on, it will start as a to-do item. Then you separate it in your agenda. Let's say it can take as long as ten minutes to get ready, but you set yourself a goal of seven minutes to complete it. With your new mindset, you will start working faster and sharper on it. Maybe, in the end, it took you eight minutes to complete, but at least you shortened the time spent on it. This self-pressure can make you more efficient at completing an activity by a certain deadline.

By the way, it has been proven that 45 minutes is a prudent time to focus on something without losing attention or getting tired, so try to put no more than 45 minutes toward completing a task.

If you have to, at least try to include a 15-minute break afterward. It will re-energize you and give you more will to finish. Such breaks should be part of your daily schedule. You should include a 15-minute break in the morning and a 15-minute break in the afternoon. Most of us already know this, but we don't do it, and we forget that it comes with benefits: it breaks your sedentary position, refreshes your mind so you feel less tired, and helps you avoid eye fatigue.

Breaks will make you more productive and healthier, so if you used to take them but no longer do, bring them back.

2) Book some spare time in case something happens. For example, I book 30 minutes of catch-up time twice a week in case I am delayed by something so I can use that spare time to compensate for it.

3) If you don't finish an activity in the time you've scheduled for it, negotiate your agenda. This means you can cut a task, search for a new time to finish your current task, or extend the time you've allotted for it, but make sure you leave enough time for the next task. For example, if you have "Update Price List" from 9:00 to 9:30 am and "Check Emails" from 9:30 to 10:00 am but you need 15 minutes more for "Update Price List," then quickly check for another 15 min in your agenda to fit the "Check Emails" timeframe previously assigned.

4) Use the Pareto rule of 20/80 to prioritize your Timebox. This means you should prioritize the 20% of activities that will accomplish 80% of your work. The rest can be assigned as you prefer.

By the way, at the beginning of this year, did you write your New Year's resolution? Could you make it work? Well, you should not miss the next chapter, where I crack the code for how to do this.

Meanwhile, if you want to learn more about Timeboxing, there is a lot of information on the internet, and I encourage you to put it into practice. Famous people like Bill Gates and Elon Musk use Timebox management with great results. And as Tarjei Vesaas, one of Norway's greatest writers, said, "Almost nothing need be said when you have eyes." So, if you have eyes on your calendar or agenda, you will definitely be more prepared for your day.

Reviewing your day is the fifth and last habit of the second block of Morning Zen.

To sum up, for your Morning Zen, you will wake up with no alarm, take your Morning Concoction, meditate, play your Happy Healthy Music, make your bed, sing, dance, and take a shower. Once you get out of the shower, you will your bed has been made, resulting in a more ordered room, a proud room. Then you will check your agenda minutes before dressing for the day. Now you are the emperor of your day; you know in advance how your day will go, and if that were not enough, you will be dressed correctly for it.

CHAPTER 13

FORGET THE NEW YEAR'S RESO-
LUTION

Morning Zen

Adrian Gonzalez

Instagram: @the_morning_zen

CHAPTER 13

FORGET THE NEW YEAR'S

RESOLUTION

When practicing Morning Zen, you will soon notice that there is a mix of great habits in this seamless routine, almost everything that can be integrated in your mornings so you can have the mindset for an amazing day. For example, it comes with peace, health, order, preparation, focus, energy, a cellphone detox, and time for you, and now we will include the steps to achieve the goals you have in mind and want to make happen.

Having goals is an important part of life because, if we don't, we enter into a comfort zone, and as a result, we don't grow. And people without goals in life tend to miss that inside energy that pushes us every morning to stand up and look out for that new project, desire, or aspiration.

Most people know Arnold Schwarzenegger as the Austrian big guy who ended up in America and found success. But the true story is that, ever since he was a kid, he had a vision.

As a boy, Arnold dreamed of living in America and becoming rich and famous, but he would never get to that if he didn't have a series of goals to achieve.

By watching documentaries and reading magazines, he found the way to define his plan. If, as a teenager, he trained hard in bodybuilding, he could compete in Austria and then win a European bodybuilding contest. Then he could go to London to compete in an international bodybuilding championship, Mr. Universe. If he won that, then he could go to America. Once there, he could continue his bodybuilding career and study acting. And if he studied acting, he could turn into an action hero. And once he turned into an action hero, he could become rich and famous.

And guess what? It wasn't easy, but he did it all. And if you ask Arnold what his secret was, he could explain it with several rules, but the main one is that he had smaller goals leading up to a bigger one, a vision.

People with goals are more motivated in life, with direction and determination, and they make better personal choices. So, take a few minutes right now to think about what your goals are. Maybe you already have, but you haven't put them down in a visible list, so take a few minutes to recall them.

In fact, have you ever made a list at the beginning of the year of personal goals that you want to achieve? And after writing these New Year's resolutions, did you fail to complete several tasks on the list and end up dropping most of them? Don't worry, you're not the only one. I did, too, year after year, until I put into action this next secret that I am about to share with you.

But before we define what personal goals we will work on, let me explain how we function. For this, let me introduce you to the **co-***fourfecta*, which includes three things all humans perform: feeling, thinking, and doing. To put it more tangibly, the points correspond with our heart, brain, and actions. The magic occurs when they all work together, but we are often unable to align them.

When we connect our brain or what we think to our actions, it is called coherence. When we think about something and then act on it, we are being coherent with what we think and do. Or, to look at it the opposite way, when someone says something but then doesn't act accordingly, they are being incoherent. So, the link between thought and action is coherence.

Now, when we connect our heart with our actions, it could be called convenience. This does not mean that being convenient is a bad thing; on the contrary, it's a way of telling ourselves that we are making a decision because we need to thrive or survive. In fact, the Merriam-Webster dictionary defines the word "convenience" as the suitability for performing an action or fulfilling a requirement. And when we connect our heart with our actions, we are fulfilling a requirement for us, for a beloved one, or in favor of a cause that we feel or believe in.

Believe it or not, we are born hardwired to survive and do things for our convenience. For example, think about your son, daughter, or any little child. When it comes time to share their toys or snack with other kids, they often say no or simply protect their things and refuse. Then an adult has to explain to them why it's important that they share. The child may or may not agree, but in the end, this sharing thing usually has to be taught. This is because our default is not to share, and this sharing process comes with education. Being protective, with a topping of egoism, is part of our DNA, and it is through education and civilization that we grow and develop to the contrary. With this, you can see how we connect our heart to our actions: we act according to **convenience**.

The third connection is between the brain and heart, and it's called being **conscious**. When you feel something and start asking yourself about it, you are becoming more conscious.

Sometimes human beings are defined as reasonable people with emotions, but we are totally the opposite. The correct definition is that **human beings are emotional people who reason**. In other words, our guts or emotions release our actions, but we have a microsecond to stop, think, and reason so we are conscious of the moment or situation we are passing through, which allows us to act consciously. So, by aligning what we feel with what we think, we are **conscious**.

But there is a fourth important part of this co-*fourfecta*: **time**. Time is the axis that will measure the duration and persistence needed to accomplish the goal, and it can be translated as **consistency**.

Let me explain them further. If we use all three, heart, brain, and actions, and set a deadline to complete it, then that is what we call setting a goal, and if we strive to complete it for an extended period, it becomes **co**nsistent. With consistency and order comes discipline, and with great discipline, you can accomplish that goal you are striving for.

For example, let's say you want to have a great body. The first step will be to connect what you want with what you think, meaning heart with brain, making you conscious of the situation. Then you will turn your thoughts into actions, such as by signing up to a gym, hiring a personal trainer, or dieting. When you take these actions every day, following a fixed schedule, you become coherent.

Finally, when you begin to see changes and enjoy the results of your sacrifices, you connect your heart to your actions, and you will start to notice your personal convenience, and if you do all this for a long period, you will be consistent. Without knowing it, you are aligned and performing this co-fourfecta for that goal, which can lead to discipline.

I'm not saying that this is the formula to become disciplined, nor that with this co-fourfecta plus discipline, you will reach your goal right away, but if one of these four characteristics is missing (conscious, coherent, convenient, and consistent), you will not have the personal foundation to reach your goal.

Now, you may be asking, "Then what are the characteristics of achieving a goal and being successful?" Well, the co-fourfecta is what you need to align on your inside so you can pursue that goal. But to be successful, you will need to excel in a mix of things: talent, discipline, deliberate practice, time spent pursuing the goal, self-care, and a touch of luck. But that is a topic I will write more about in my next book, which I encourage you to read as well.

When we add a new goal to our New Year's resolutions, it goes from our heart to our brain, but with the passage of the time, our resolve begins to lose strength. Our actions become inconsistent, we start failing in one or more areas of the co-fourfecta, and we end up dropping it.

But no worries. I will share a secret with you. The key process in Morning Zen is to make sure you remember to include the co-fourfecta for the goal you are pursuing.

We will include it this way. What is that thing you want in life and are passionate about (convenient)? What if you wrote that goal down and read it every day (conscious)? And then you added exactly how you are going to achieve it (coherent)? And on top of that, what would happen if, every morning, you read this step-by-step process, meaning the how and the why of what you are doing, until it becomes a habit (consistent)?

But let's think bigger. What would happen if you applied this constant reading to all the areas you want to improve in your life? And on top of that, what if you did this on a daily basis? You won't even notice it, but you will be performing a Manifesto—your Manifesto.

So, the next time you make a New Year's resolution, forget about the classic way of doing it, writing a list of your goals. In fact, forget about it completely. Instead, I invite you to write it in a new way, one that includes how you are going to complete these tasks and why you will pursue them, and that will be your Manifesto.

Remember that this will be the paper that you will be reading every morning. This means it is important to have this paper or note nearby, such as on your nightstand, and that you read it every time you can (laminate it, if necessary). By doing this, you are creating the quirk of repeating to yourself all the processes you are working on, like a type of auto-coaching, implying that If we read it every day, two things may happen.

One is that, since you are repeating your course of action every day in your mind, you will start taking actions to achieve your goal, and in the end, you will reach it. And in case you have a relapse or miss a day, by reading it again, you will encourage yourself to resume your actions.

The second is the worst-case scenario: you may stop reading it because you realize that you are not going to do what you proposed. In other words, you cannot torture yourself by reading a process that you are not performing. We cannot allow this, so in the next chapter, I will talk more about it.

As a personal check-up, what this could mean is that the co-fourfecta is not aligned, meaning you are no longer thinking, acting, feeling, or consistent about it. You will have to verify why this is and realign yourself for the goal you want to achieve.

But the good news is, once you have realigned, by reading your plan every day, you will unconsciously find a way to start working on that goal again.

co-fourfecta we talked about.

We all should have a Manifesto. That is what this next chapter is about: writing down your Manifesto and reading it every morning during Morning Zen. So, go get a pen and paper or your nearest electronic device and join me in the next chapter, where I explain how to create your personal manifesto.

To sum up on this chapter, I would like to share the following phrase from the former Mr. Olympia, Conan, the one who killed Predator, the Terminator, the governor of California, the one who told us, "I'll be back," and who wisely stated:

"If you don't have a vision of where you go, and if you don't have a goal of where you go, you drift around and you never end up anywhere."

–Arnold Schwarzenegger

Now, let's go and write your Manifesto.

CHAPTER 14

MANIFESTO

Morning Zen

Adrian Gonzalez

Instagram: @the_morning_zen

CHAPTER 14

MANIFESTO

For those of you asking where I got this Manifesto practice, I have to confess that it was from the great book *Think and Grow Rich* by Napoleon Hill. If you get the opportunity to read it, you will learn a lot from it. Among the many things that this fantastic book talks about, the one that impacted me the most was the Manifesto, where he encourages having one and explains how to make one.

In this Manifesto, Napoleon Hill invites us to write down the important things we want in life. He emphasizes that you need to include the process, and he stresses the importance of reading it several times every day.

After a couple of years of practicing this Manifesto reading, I saw an opportunity to include other things in life. So, I will share with you how to write your Manifesto with a mix of Napoleon Hill and Adrian Gonzalez. This means it is not only entrepreneur-rich-oriented, but also works for personal growth.

However, I want to make clear that Napoleon Hill's version of the Manifesto is great, and if you want to use it, go ahead. I encourage you to buy and read this book. I think it is amazing, and it helped me for many years in my life.

Your Manifesto should be focused on just one major goal, and it could be anything you are pursuing: starting a new business, losing weight, forming a family, getting rich, you name it. But it must be just one topic. It should not be longer than a sheet of letter-size paper. Write your goal down, print it, and have it near your bed. Print a second copy for your office, where you can read it every day. If it's possible, read it three times a day, in the morning, afternoon, and night.

Like your intentions, the Manifesto has to be written in the present tense, like it's about to occur at any time. In other words, try to use the verb "going" rather than "will." Additionally, this Manifesto will contain six short

paragraphs covering the main concept, the how, reinforcement, visualization, and personal environment.
And without more to say, here is the Manifesto structure.

In the first paragraph, you will write your main goal
and the date you want it to reach it. Remember, a dream
with a deadline becomes a goal, so a date is always necessary. As Walt Disney said, "Everyone needs deadlines...
If we didn't have deadlines, we'd stagnate."

So, let's say that your Manifesto includes the goal that
you want to be entrepreneur-rich; it's not enough to just
write that you want to be rich. Instead, you need to be
more specific and write down exactly how much money
you want, the specific date by which this goal will come
true, and how acquiring it will take place. For example, if
your goal is losing weight, write down how many pounds
you want to lose, the specific day you will achieve your
weight loss goal, and how this reduction will take place.
Try to use no more than three lines to do this.

In the second paragraph, you will describe the process
that will help you perform it. Using the example above,
you will describe how you will lose weight and the process you will follow to do it: how you will go to the gym,
at what time you will arrive, your training schedule, the
routines you will perform, the diet you will follow, and so

on.

And if your Manifesto is entrepreneur-rich-oriented, you will describe how you will get this money and the process by which it will manifest in your life. For example, "In exchange, I am providing this service/product..." In this case, you would also include what makes your product or service unique and what you want your customers to perceive so they are satisfied, recommend your product or service, and want more from your company.

Finally, in this same paragraph, include the steps you will take to make this happen. For example: "I'm starting to appreciate eating my diet food, and I'm hiring a personal trainer" or "I'm hiring the correct people for my team, and then I am going to train them with the best sales trainer. Then they will be selling like crazy, making my product one of the most consumed in the market. Customers are going to love it..."

Now, you might be asking, "What is the purpose of this paragraph?" The answer is that you will be doing a daily check of your status and aligning your vision with your reality, and by reading this plan every day, you will be on top of it, knowing where in the process you are, and in case you are delayed or stuck, you will work smarter to finish that step so you can continue with the next one.

The third paragraph is the reinforcement, meaning, if it is losing weight, you will describe the slow process of the results that you will start noticing, in other words, you will focus on the convenience. And if it is entrepreneur-rich-oriented, describe the type of customer you want to consume your product or service. Also, describe how you would like your company to be seen by the rest of the world and your non-negotiable values.

The focus of the fourth paragraph is faith and visualization. If you are working on losing weight, then describe here how you visualize yourself when you reach your goal. This will feed your desire to continue working your weight loss plan. And in case your main goal is to be entrepreneur-rich, write out your vision for how this will happen. For example, "I can visualize how my savings accounts are going to increase..." Also express your faith and conviction that your vision will happen.

In the fifth paragraph, you will write down your personal environment and all the things you want to improve to be a better person, reinforce your values, etc. For example, "I will read a book on business. I will eat healthier and commit to being a better boss, love partner, etc." And make sure to finish this paragraph with a phrase that says something like this: "... and all this will be accomplished through persistence and the faith I have in myself and my almighty God. Amen." Respectfully, I'm not a religious person, but I consider myself a spiritual being and believe that God never abandons us. This final line will be a premium seal, making sure we include God in our plan. And if you are an atheist, that's ok. In that case, just substitute the universe or whatever fits with your beliefs.

There is a great sixth paragraph, and in the next chapter, I will explain what goes in it. For now, save at least four lines at the end of the page to include it. However, these first paragraphs are the main ones for your Manifesto.

You will read your Manifesto every day during Morning Zen, and it will focus on the main goal you want to achieve in the middle or long term. By reading it every day, you will remind yourself of that goal you want so much and the steps you need to take to reach it. This means it will no longer be just a wish; you will be thinking about it and repeating it to yourself every day, ensuring that you stay on track.

So, write down that goal, that dream, that thing that you want so much, and read it every day until you achieve it. And to make sure that we do this, we are including it as part of the habits in Morning Zen. That way, it will be a part of your daily reading every morning of your life.

As I mentioned before, the magic of this book is that you can immediately put into practice what you get from it. When we read something and don't put it into practice, we soon forget it, and that knowledge does not grow. On the other hand, when we learn something new and put it into practice right away, we use parts of the brain that help us perform this new learning, so it sticks in our memory, turning knowledge into savvy. Try to always jump from reading a book to practicing what's in it or talking about it. If you do, you will notice a better understanding of the subject you are learning.

As I said before, we need to argue with the experience, so it's important that you pick up a pen and paper right now or go to your electronic device and write your Manifesto. It doesn't have to be perfect; just write it, print it, display it, and have it ready to include in your Morning Zen.

Reading your Manifesto is the first habit of the third and last block of Morning Zen.

Anyhow, if you want to know more about how I read my Manifesto, continue to the next chapter, where I will explain the magic of having one.

But right now, don't procrastinate. Count down, three, two, one, and start writing your Manifesto immediately.

CHAPTER 15

THE MORNING COFFEE

COMPANY

Morning Zen

Adrian Gonzalez

Instagram: @the_morning_zen

CHAPTER 15

THE MORNING COFFEE COMPANY

The best way to review your Morning Zen Manifesto is to enjoy a cup of coffee, tea, or other drink as you read it. In this chapter, we will explain why.

Before I explain the coffee concept, let me introduce some rules for your Manifesto you started to write, so we can eliminate doubt and you can feel more comfortable with it. First, **your Manifesto does not have to be "*perfecto*"**. It just needs to help you recall the goal you are pursuing.

Second, it is flexible, meaning you can edit and modify it as many times as you want to for as long as you want to. Our tastes and goals change over time. For example, think about your favorite color when you were a kid. Maybe it was pink or blue, but now that you are a grown adult with more life experiences, maybe it is no longer your favorite. This can happen with your goals, too, meaning, once you finish achieving them, you will probably find new ones to pursue, or it could be that you will discover that the personal environment you were working in is no longer what you need. As time passes, it's ok to change priorities or steps as long as you are in tune with them.

Third, the Manifesto comes first, before your actions. When you read your Manifesto, you might be stuck and unable to move on to the next step described in it, causing you frustration and making you want to drop reading it. Don't stop. Instead, take a moment to think about why you are unable to complete the steps that are there and then change the actions. In other words, change the hows but do not quit your goals nor stop reading your Manifesto.

Fourth, try to make it short and sweet, less than one side of a sheet of paper. Remember that our focus is inversely proportional to the amount of time that has passed. This means that, if your Manifesto is too long, the chances that you will start losing focus or thinking about other things while reading it is high.

Fifth, read your Manifesto while enjoying your favorite morning drink. In other words, if you like to drink juice, tea, or coffee in the morning, that is the perfect moment to read the Manifesto because it ties the habit to an enjoyable activity. Do it, and you will see what I mean by this.

Some of you might now be asking, "Adrian, how, exactly, do you read your Manifesto?" Well, I have the following routine for breakfast. First, I prepare a little bowl of fruit, which usually includes bananas, papaya, apples, pears, or pineapple. Then I make a slice of wholemeal toast. To drink, I make a glass of 50% orange juice and 50% water to get all the benefits of the orange and the necessary water to hydrate. Finally, I take some vitamins and finish up with a delicious cup of Panamanian Geisha coffee.

The Panamanian Geisha is a high-end coffee that grows in the high lands of Boquete, Province of Chiriqui, Republic of Panama, and it is considered one of the best coffees in the world, with hints of berry, lemon, orange, grapefruit, mango, peach, papaya, pineapple, guava, and other fruits, depending on the bean.

It has won many awards outside the region, and depending on where you are getting it, it can be one of the most expensive coffees in the world. So, if you are a coffee lover like me, I invite you to try Panama Geisha Coffee. If the price is a limitation, no worries, if you come to visit Panama, you can surely get one at an attractive price.

And in case you ask me, "Adrian, does there is a distinct collection or brand you recommend?" Well, I have to confess that part of the pages written of this book, took place in a cozy coffee shop, located in Vía Argentina, Panama City, Panama, where they have a selection, I consider one of my top coffees to drink. And it's the Geisha Coffee of **Mentiritas Blancas.**

In fact, let me share a secret with you. If you go there, please ask for the Geisha Experience, where a well train barista, will meticulously brew you an exquisite geisha coffee, in a distinct cup of wine, so you can slowly swirl it, and all the while appreciate its fruitful properties in aroma, richness and flavor that emanates from this delicious gourmet coffee. And guess which are the two words I'm about to say? Yes -highly recommended.

By the way, if is your first time, don't kill it with milk. Meaning, for regular purpose, I like to drink my coffee served as cappuccino, which comes with milk. But if you want to appreciate the real taste of a Geisha Coffee, if you add milk, you will neutralize part of its flavor and won't be able to appreciate all the kindness that comes with this brew.

If you come and visit Panama and would like to appreciate a great coffee, get some inspiration, or meet with friends, please put in your agenda, *go and visit* the Geisha Experience at Mentiritas Blancas, and you will understand what I mean with this.

Giancarlo, if you are reading this, my greetings.

Let's go back to the original question, how do I read my Manifesto? Well, once I finish my breakfast, I take my coffee cup in one hand and my Manifesto in the other, and I proceed to read it aloud while drinking my delicious Geisha.

Last but not least is a delicate part where you need to be conscious of your routine. While reading the Manifesto, grab the phone and knock out the things you need to perform your Manifesto. Why is this delicate? Because you will be using your phone, but you are still doing Morning Zen, so you should not get involved with your messages or any app that will capture your attention.

And what do I mean by knocking out the things in your Manifesto? Well, for example, let's say that your Manifesto has a step that says, "I will find a personal trainer so he can guide me with my routine," and you are in the process of checking the prices of personal trainer services so you can decide which one to go with. So, you will grab the phone and send the message right away, with no distractions, to the service providers so they can reply to you with the prices you need to make a decision.

Don't worry or wait for the response, just shoot, and they will respond when they can. And in case they respond right away, do not open the message. Instead, leave it and follow up once you finish your Morning Zen.

By doing this, and with the help of the Manifesto, you are doing the steps you need to follow up on for the goal you are pursuing. And this can apply to all the steps in your Manifesto that need follow-up.

Remember, send messages that are short and quick. Don't wait for the response. Instead, turn down your phone and continue reading the Manifesto, and if there is another step that needs to be followed up on, repeat the same process. But remember the golden rule: don't get distracted by the other things on your phone.

There is also a bright side to the Manifesto. You might

not believe it, but the Manifesto provides a few rewards. As time passes, you will sense tiny peaks of satisfaction while reading it. This is because you will start noticing that some of the steps you wrote have been accomplished, which means you are getting closer to your goal and it can be done.

If you are curious about the science behind reading a goal every day and want to know where the inspiration for this Manifesto comes from and if it works, here is a real-world example.

As I mentioned before, I like to watch La Liga Española, with a bit of an inclination to support the Real Madrid Football Club, considered one of the best soccer clubs in the world. On July 1, 2009, Real Madrid acquired one of the best strikers in the world from Manchester United, Cristiano Ronaldo dos Santos Aveiro, also known as CR7. If you look closely, this guy is a reflection of what I mean by success. He had talent and discipline, engaged in deliberate practice and self-care, dedicated time to improving his skills, and had a touch of luck. The result is that he won more awards and broke more records than anyone else of his time.

If you ask me what thought Cristiano Ronaldo repeated over and over to himself while growing up and throughout his career, well, I am convinced that it was: "I am going to be the biggest football player in the world."

That thought must have been pounding and repeating in his mind since he was a kid, let's say six years old. And after years of repeating it, practicing, and putting effort into his goal, he won his first *Ballon d'Or* in 2008.

The *Ballon d'Or* is the FIFA "Golden Ball" given to soccer players who have performed the best in all FIFA competitions for that year and have a great presence in the UEFA Champions League.

This league is an annual soccer competition organized by the Union of European Football Associations (UEFA) and contested by top-division European clubs. The competition winners are decided through group and knock-out format. In other words, it's where the best soccer clubs of Europe compete.

The soccer team with the most championships so far is Real Madrid. After Cristiano Ronaldo won his first Golden Ball at the age of 23, they acquired him.

Perhaps Cristiano Ronaldo did not have a Manifesto that he read every day, but I'm convinced that he has not stopped repeating that same phrase of being the best soccer player in the world, day after day, since he went on to accumulate numerous cups, trophies, and records during his time as a professional player.

Something similar happened to former American professional boxer Mike Tyson early in his career. His father figure and trainer, Constantine D'Amato, always repeated to him, "You are gonna be world champion."

And what about Russian chess grandmaster and former world chess champion Garry Kasparov? When he was young, his mother put a big sign on the wall of his room that said: "If you don't, who?"

So, instead of remembering the phrase for the goal you want to achieve, you will read it every day during Morning Zen until you achieve it. And remember, you are not just repeating the goal; you are reading through the process, which will encourage you to take the steps needed to reach the goal, your goal.

As American author and international lecturer Dr. Joe Dispenza says, "If you are not defined by a vision of the future, you are left with the memories of the past, and people believe more in their past that what they should believe in their future." Having a Manifesto will make you work to define your vision, pursue your goals, and believe in your future.

You should take into consideration that the purpose of your Manifesto is to focus on a dream with a deadline, meaning a date by which it will be achieved, because, once you put a date to a dream, it turns into a goal. If you divide that goal into steps, it turns into a plan. If the plan is supported by actions and those actions include going over the goal each day as a habit, it will turn into reality.

So, to sum up, you will wake up with no alarm, go quickly to the kitchen and drink your Morning Concoction, meditate, delay hedonic adaptation by writing down the things you are grateful for, put down your daily intentions, send them to the universe, pump up the volume with your wake-up playlist, make your bed, sing, dance, take a shower, review your schedule as historical emperors did, get dressed to impress, finish your breakfast, drink your coffee while reading your Manifesto, and voilà, you are locked and loaded for the next chapter.

CHAPTER 16

THE ONE

THAT MULTIPLIES

Morning Zen

Adrian Gonzalez

Instagram: @the_morning_zen

CHAPTER 16

THE ONE THAT MULTIPLIES

"People may hear your words, but they feel your attitude."

—John C. Maxwell

In this chapter, I would like to share a lesson given by the great Spanish university professor Victor Küppers in 2013 during his Andoralla Vella TED talk on how you can determine the value of a person. In other words, how much are you worth as a person? He did it by sharing the following story.

One day, he was about to go on vacation with his family to the beach, and he checked out a hotel that had repeatedly been recommended in his Twitter account. He visited the hotel website, but guess what? There were no pictures at all, so he wrote an email to the hotel asking for pictures because, as he said, "I don't know about your partner, but my wife, if she does not see pictures, I cannot convince her." For his wife, pictures had the most meaning, so no pictures, no trip. Hahaha.

This is a great Ted talk that you must see on YouTube. Just type "Victor Küppers Attitude Ted." It lasts 20:05 minutes. It's in Spanish, but you can put on the closed caption feature in the settings, and the subtitles for English will be shown, making it easier to understand.

So, back to Victor's story. When he got the reply from the hotel, he could not believe the great response and amazing attitude of the woman who responded, and he appreciated all the pictures she took with her personal cellphone, including the pictures needed to convince his wife to stay at that hotel. And she ended the email by saying, "If you need more pictures, don't worry. I can go back and take more. Just ask."

Küppers was happy yet annoyed by her answer, and in his talk, he gives a formula to calculate the value of a person, $V = (K+S) \times A$, where V stands for value, meaning how much worth a person has, not from a financial standpoint but as a human being, K stands for knowledge, meaning all the education and knowledge that you have, and S stands for skill, the ability or experience one has with a certain discipline, work, or task.

For example, let's say you want to determine the value of a person who has a lot of knowledge but no ability. Going further, let's say it is a student who has recently finished college. He has knowledge but little experience or talent in his field ($K\uparrow + S\downarrow$). For an entry position that person will fit.

But on the other hand, maybe a person is hired because of his ability and skills but has no technical education in the subject ($K\downarrow + S\uparrow$), like a skilled person with no degree. For example, a company might hire a young guy who knows a lot about computers but has no college or computer science degree. However, because of his skill and talent in the subject, he is worthy of the job.

But as Victor says, you need knowledge to do anything. To serve beer properly, knowledge is needed. To work as a financier, knowledge is needed. Just as important are skills and experience, which count a lot when it comes to doing anything.

However, there is an important variable in this formula: the A, which stands for attitude. And as you can see from the formula, guess what? Knowledge adds, and skill adds—but **attitude multiplies**: V= (K+S) x A.

As Victor says, people who think you are an amazing person, that you certainly are, do so because of your way of being. Appreciation does not come from what you know or the degrees and titles you have. Appreciation does not come from your skills or the years you've put into your career. People appreciate each other because of their way of being.

Let's put it this way. All fantastic people have a fantastic way of being, and all the miserable people we meet have a miserable way of being. And guess what? This applies to bosses, too. If you had to pick which former boss to work for, which one would you choose, the fantastic one or the miserable one?

This doesn't mean that knowledge and skill are not important. In fact, Küppers emphasizes that knowledge is very important, and skill is also vital, but what differentiates a crack from a racket is the attitude, the ability to communicate, to work as a team, to be cheerful, optimistic, enthusiastic, and effort maker. But I can guarantee you that we won't choose to go back to work for a former boss because of their knowledge. Instead, it will be because of their way of being.

If we look at it on a personal level, this is even easier to see. How do we select our friends? By knowledge, skills, or attitude? Nobody chooses friends because of their resume or LinkedIn account. We select them because of their way of being.

But the issue is, when we feel discouraged, we lose the most important thing that we have: our attitude. We don't lose knowledge or experience, but our amazing attitude. To understand how devastating this can be, think about a doctor in a hospital. Let's say that this doctor has all the knowledge and skill he needs, but he has one big weakness: his awful attitude with his colleagues and how pessimistic he is with his patients, A=↓, so how would you rate that doctor? You'd say he was senseless and awful.

Now, remember how, at the beginning of this book, I mentioned that I would talk about my brother? Well, here is where he enters the story. My brother, Dr. Arkel Gonzalez, is a well-known doctor in Panama who specializes in orthopedics and trauma. Inside this orthopedic world, he sub-specializes in foot and ankle problems. So, if you have a sprained ankle, fractured a toe, or developed a bunion, he is the guy you go to.

When Dr. Arkel is with his patients, besides focusing

on transmitting his knowledge or the action plan he recommends for the treatment, he adopts a natural disposition that makes his patients open to confiding in him, making them feel more relaxed in case they need surgery. He builds that confidence with his amazing attitude. Let me explain how he does it.

When consulting with a patient, before he gets into why they came to visit him, Dr. Arkel first tries to establish a rapport. But this is not the trite rapport one might build with customers by understanding them and being empathic. It's more than that.

It is about using that rapport to put the patient at ease. In other words, he does a quick check of the patient and, by instinct, perceives what type of conversation he can begin with. From there, he moves from topic to topic in a seamless way until he finds a point in common, like a hobby, sport, or common interest that they can talk about.

Indeed, sometimes he includes some funny stories that just happened to him, showing the patient his human side. This makes the patient let go of any pressure, fear, or uncertainty, so when they jump to the reason for their medical visit, they automatically feel more comfortable speaking about it. For him, seeing a patient is not a clinical consultation, but more like a friend-to-friend conversation. And as a friend, it's easier for the patient to explain exactly what's wrong.

He once told me about a time when the entire city trembled because of an earthquake. A few days later, a patient visited, and as they conversed, the subject of the earthquake came up. So, my brother tells the patient about his experience during the earthquake. He was on the top floor of the building, and everything started to move. The lights shook, the tables shuddered, and the sound of things rocking make him run at full speed to the nearest exit. When he made it out of the building, he was consumed with fear. A couple of nurses were there, and they stared at him, as they could see how afraid he was. Then, out of the blue, the nurses started laughing at how afraid he looked and because of the irony that they were all women but were totally relaxed. The patient laughed at the story, too, and then he started to tell Dr. Arkel about his own experience during the earthquake. In this way, Dr. Arkel's attitude multiplied his worth beyond his knowledge and skills.

This is a one-of-a-kind attitude because it's authentic, and his patients love him for it. Actually, I once asked him how he knows if his patients are happy with him after surgery or treatment. In response, he told me about the *grocery meter*. "The what?" I asked, just as you are probably thinking right now. "What do you mean by the *grocery meter?*"

He explained, "Sometimes my wife calls me after work to see if I can stop at the grocery store to buy some food she needs for dinner. So, as a smart husband who listens to his wife, I go and do it because, if I forget, I will spend my night sleeping on the couch. In the grocery store, I sometimes see a surgery patient of mine in the distance. And because I know my wife is waiting for me, I try to focus on finding what she requested, purchasing it, and getting home as soon as possible.

But then comes the *grocery meter*. That is when the patient sees me, recognizes me, and heads my way to salute me and start a conversation. That is the meter where I can say that I did something right. It could be due to the surgery, the recommendation, the rapport, or the connection that I had with the patient, but that salute reminds me why I'm a doctor and how my service can make other people happier at certain points in their lives."

In my opinion, my brother's secret is the attitude he transmits to his patients from day one. Now, you might be asking me, "Adrian, do they love him?" Well, I can tell you that after he finishes a patient's treatment, they often bring him things like chickens, vegetables, or fruits from their farms as thanks. And guess what one patient gave him as a present? It was a big sack of recently harvested Geisha coffee beans from one of the best coffee estates in the Boquete region.

If you would like to know more about Dr. Arkel, he has several videos on YouTube about bones and injuries. If you have a moment, check them out. Just search for "Dr. Arkel" on YouTube, and you will find them. I am certain you will enjoy his channel.

Now, the good news about all this learning is that a positive attitude can be developed and practiced. To find out to pump up your attitude in the morning, follow me to the next chapter, "The Five Pillars." Two words: highly recommended.

CHAPTER 17

THE FIVE PILLARS

Morning Zen

Adrian Gonzalez

Instagram: @the_morning_zen

CHAPTER 17

THE FIVE PILLARS

One takeaway from the previous chapter is that we all need knowledge and skills, but the most important thing is our attitude—our attitude with relatives, friends, coworkers, customers, and direct reports. That will be the real value that they have for us.

But the amazing part of that formula is that it can take time to acquire knowledge and skill, but not attitude. Changing our attitude can take as little as one second. Attitude comes from inside, so we will work on five internal pillars to help us appreciate, enjoy, and rethink ourselves, making us feel better. And guess what? If we feel good on the inside, we will project the same attitude on the outside, so these pillars make us conscious about how we feel so we project this great attitude throughout our day. And the best part is that it can be developed and practiced. And yes, it is included in Morning Zen.

As you move from pillar to pillar, you will spend about 20 to 30 seconds on each. A clock or timer won't be needed; just calculate it mentally. So, breathe, close your eyes, and follow the instructions, and your best attitude will start shining forth.

Remember when, in the previous chapter, I suggested leaving a space for the sixth paragraph in the Manifesto? Well, this is that paragraph. But before writing it down, let me explain what you have to do when you read each of these pillars.

The first breathing pillar is happiness with gratitude. As we heard before, being happy is a decision that we can choose to start our day. Ego and gratitude cannot exist at the same time, so to enforce our happiness, we need to lower our ego and expectations, which sometimes pound on our heads, making us forget to appreciate other things we have in life.

We will do this by closing our eyes, focusing on our breath, and giving thanks for our current condition. In other words, give thanks for the air you are breathing, and from there, include everything you have in your life. At that point, your brain will fill with thoughts of gratitude. Breathe deeply through this pillar and try to be in that state of gratitude for no longer than 30 seconds because then we have to jump to the next one.

Now, open your eyes and quickly read the second pillar, which is love for everything you are. You will then close your eyes again, focus on your breathing, and start remembering all the good things, why you love you. Send waves of love to yourself and repeat the following phrase: I love myself because..." Complete it with the first things that come to your mind and remain in that state for no longer than 30 seconds because then you have to jump to the next pillar.

Third is the pillar of enjoying the moments you are living right now. Maybe you are passing through a difficult change in your life. Instead of complaining about it, try to perceive it as a process to enjoy. The way you feel about the difficult circumstances you are struggling with can be improved if you change your mindset ipso facto by seeing it as a process to enjoy.

For example, a friend of mine got fired during the COVID 19 pandemic due to a reduction in the labor force. At first, he felt frustrated due to all the time he'd dedicated to the company, but when he began to practice Morning Zen, he realized that, instead of complaining, he could take dedicate his free time to a personal project, spend more time with his family, and reorganize his life. And he did this by changing his attitude in a second and reinforcing this mindset in his breathing pillars during Morning Zen.

Recently he told me that he feels happier than before and enjoys his life more due to this positive attitude, which consists of focusing his energy on enjoying the present moment.

Once you read this pillar, close your eyes, breathe, and start thinking about all those things that are occurring in your life. Then repeat and complete the phrase: "I am enjoying the process of..." Stay there for no longer than 30 seconds and then jump to the next one.

The fourth breathing pillar is bringing out your passion for that thing you love and do daily. Let's say you are an accountant, a manager, or a company director. In this space, start looking inside yourself for the passion you have for the numbers, managing people, decision-making, or work that you love to do. Awake that energy inside yourself and begin to recall why you are so passionate about it.

The difference between a passionate and miserable person is that the passionate person, instead of complaining, seeks love in the task or job that he is doing, and he can sense it. So, breathe, close your eyes, and complete the following phrase: "I am passionate about..." Stay there for no longer than 30 seconds before jumping to the last one.

Once you open your eyes, read the Fifth Breathing Pillar: "I am ready to receive the good things that are for me." Sometimes things are out in the world for us, but we cannot see them because we don't attract them or express our intent to acquire them.

One way of doing this is to communicate to the universe that we are ready to receive those good things in life that are out there waiting for us. And with this breathing comes a physical pose: spread your arms wide, lift your chin a bit, and send that vibration to the universe, expressing mentally that you are ready to receive what it has to offer.

So, close your eyes and do this for about 30 seconds. Communicate to the universe that you are ready to receive the good things out there for you.

I like to end this breathing phase with a quote by Tony Robins but with one little word changed. So, Tony, if you are reading this, my greetings, and thanks for the quote and your inspiration. The quote I like to end with is "Energy grows where attention goes."

And with this, you end the Five Breathing Pillars for a positive attitude. Afterward, you will notice a positive change, or at least you will reset your mindset and have a positive and energized mood to start the day.

Now, maybe you think that we are repeating meditation with this step, but it is different. For one thing, it is shorter, meaning you don't enter a deep state of mind. It has moments when you have to open your eyes to read a Breath Pillar and guide yourself. And instead of thinking about nothing, you are focusing on five elements that will make you have the best attitude every day for the rest of your life.

If you are asking how to insert all of this in the sixth paragraph of the Manifesto, no worries. I already thought about it. I've written the following lines, and you can copy and paste them.

Now I will close my eyes and think about these five breathing pillars: 1) Gratitude for breathing this air and all the things I have. 2) Love for everything I am. 3) Enjoying all the moments that I am living right now. 4)

Passion for everything I do. 5) I am ready to receive all the good things to come. "Energy grows where attention goes."

Performing the five breath pillars is the second habit of the third block of Morning Zen.

And with this suitable mojo to close your Manifesto, you are almost ready to end your Morning Zen.

CHAPTER 18

IS IT FOR LIFE?

Morning Zen

Adrian Gonzalez

Instagram: @the_morning_zen

CHAPTER 18

IS IT FOR LIFE?

Before getting to the next interesting chapter, "My Other Best Practices," I would like to help you clear doubts about how long Morning Zen should be and if it should be performed 365 days of the year. To answer these questions, Morning Zen should be performed as part of your daily work routine. This means you should only do it on the days you have to work and can take a break on the weekends.

And how long should you do it? Well, Morning Zen is designed so you can succeed at the things you can control, meaning, as long as you want to be successful, you should perform it. It's like going to the gym. If you want to stay fit, you have to do it for life. The same is true for Morning Zen.

The good news is that, once you master it, you can include new goals, modify your Manifesto, change meditations, and add new music, all as a part of your daily start. There may be days when, because of a major change, trip, urgency, or new shift, the practice of Morning Zen could be affected. As with every discipline in life, try to reintegrate it into your daily routine as soon as you can. And if you like Morning Zen, I would appreciate it if you would spread the word and talk about it. Thank you in advance.

So, what about other habits? I'm sure that while you were reading this book, a couple of other habits and ideas began to cross your mind. If you are asking, "May I include one of them?" Well, the answer is, why not? You can include steps, add new habits, or adapt Morning Zen to a discipline or a practice you were already performing. As long as it brings positive results in your life, respects the phone detox period, and you can perform it under your control, then it is totally welcome.

And what about physical activity? People may be asking why I didn't include an exercise routine in Morning Zen, considering all the benefits of working out. The reason is that training is highly contingent on personal taste and outcome and including it might cause a conflict for people.

For example, I like to work out in a gym, while others may like to do outdoor exercises, like running or biking. If you include an exercise routine in Morning Zen, it might lead to someone overtraining or not doing it because they already have an exercise routine. But if you think that a couple of minutes of exercise can help you, add it.

As a matter of fact, a friend of mine included a set of 100 pushups plus 100 crunches. The exercise is not time-consuming, and it works fine for him.

So, in the end, it is your call. My mission is to share with you the art of effortlessly following this amazing collection of great habits during your mornings, completely in your control and in a prudent, tested time, so you can discover this new meaning of success.

Now, if you want to add another little step, benefit, or habit, that's ok; they are welcome. But remember, Morning Zen has been designed to last for a prudent amount of time so that it can easily fit into your mornings. The reality is that we all have a daily life to attend to and practicing additional routines during Morning Zen can turn it into a long morning drill, causing us to sacrifice other things or devote more of your valuable 24 hours than you have to spend.

Nevertheless, I do other habits outside of Morning Zen, what I like to call "my other best practices," and I am glad to share them with you. If they click with you, then you can practice them as well. To find out what they are, follow me to the next chapter.

CHAPTER 19

MY OTHER BEST

PRACTICES

Morning Zen

Adrian Gonzalez

Instagram: @the_morning_zen

CHAPTER 19

MY OTHER BEST PRACTICES

Let's get right to the point. Here are the other great habits that I practice outside of Morning Zen that encourage me to keep learning, inspire me, and enhance my development.

One is to listen to other things than music. Since we already have a nice period set aside during Morning Zen to listen to good music, at other times, we can listen to other things. One of these times could be when you are on your way to work.

Most of the time, when we are in a car, we listen to music as we enjoy the to our next stop, which can be our office, a meeting with a customer, etc. Instead of playing the usual music playlist, I listen to an interesting podcast. Why a podcast? Because it provides three benefits.

One is that you can learn something new. The second is the variety. Currently, there are two million podcasts, so you have plenty to choose from according to the topic you are interested in or your mood.

For example, when I am about to meet with a customer to show them a project or proposal, I like to listen to sales and customers' podcasts so I can pick up some tips beforehand.

Third is that some of them are not so long and can fit the time that it takes you to travel from one place to the next. So, feel free to try it. The next time you are heading to your office or a meeting, take advantage of that time and put on a podcast on the topic you are interested in.

Another habit is to read or watch an inspirational book or video on Sundays. Why? Because it helps us to be motivated for the rest of the week. When you read about something that you need or are interested in, for example, reading about marketing because you need some tips about that topic, your brain considers all kinds of ideas, and from there, you can find options to implement them in your work, projects, or personal plan. It also gives you the motivation to start your Mondays with the energy you need.

Reading brings ideas, and good ideas bring motivation. If you feel motivated about work on Sundays, you will start your Mondays with that boost of inspiration loaded. For example, on most Sundays, I set aside a block of reading time from 4:00 pm to 5:00 pm. My mind unconsciously knows about it, so now I do it as part of my Sunday routine. So, I recommend scheduling reading time on Sundays. Get that book you would like to learn about and start reading. Once you start this habit, you will understand what I mean.

Another option is to listen to audiobooks while training. If you are like me and like to hit the weights at the gym, instead of listening to music with your headphones, I invite you to play the audiobook of that thick book you always wanted to read but have been putting off because it's too long or you can't find the time. You can finish most books in less than a week while working out.

Another habit? Buy clothes. You may be saying, "What? You are definitely a consumerist." But no, it's not like that. Buying clothes gives you two benefits. One is that you will project that freshness of having something new to wear. The second is that this practice will help you with your self-esteem. This is not because it is a way to pamper yourself, though, in a way, it is. It's more because new clothes make you feel sharp, fresh, new, and self-loved, which, in turn, leads to greater self-esteem. This is why, when women experience a difficult situation, they go shopping; it helps them feel spoiled and more beautiful.

Now, I am not saying that you have to buy expensive clothes. But with this habit, at least you can buy a nice shirt or pair of jeans once a month with the money you would spend on a single dinner. In other words, if you eat out several times a month, sacrifice one of those meals and use the money to buy an article of clothing.

In my case, I try to buy a black t-shirt or white shirt once in a while so I can have that fresh new shirt that's ready to wear. Going further, there's nothing like wearing a brand-new white shirt for the first time. It comes with that glow, that elegance, that feeling you get when you enter a room that people can sense that you have arrived.

At the same time, you can also donate the clothes you have stopped using. Avoid accumulating clothes. When you buy new ones, you should think about what old articles of clothing you will move to your basket of clothes to donate. As you buy, you share.

Another habit I encourage is listening to positive affirmations while falling asleep. This practice is similar to the one shown in the great movie directed by John Lee Hancock called *The Founder*, where Ray Kroc, played by Michael Keaton, meets the owners of McDonald's, realizes the restaurant's potential, and makes it one of the biggest and most famous restaurants in the world.

The Ray Kroc character has a particular night habit: listening to positive affirmations while doing other things. In the movie, he carries a portable turntable everywhere he goes, and he plays a record containing a motivational speech by Calvin Coolidge called "The Power of Persistence." It starts like this:

> Nothing in this world can take the place of persistence. Talent will not; nothing is more common than unsuccessful men with talent. Genius will not; unrewarded genius is almost a proverb. Education will not; the world is full of educated derelicts. Persistence and determination alone are omnipotent. The slogan Press On! has solved and always will solve the

problems of the human race.

This movie has many lessons, but one, in particular, is that you can reprogram your unconscious state of mind with positive thoughts, and one of the best times to do this is while falling asleep. Similar to what Dr. Bruce Lipton explains. He is an American biologist who studies neuroplasticity and the subconscious mind. Neural plasticity is the ability of neurons and neural networks in the brain to change their connections and behavior in response to damage, dysfunction, new information, sensory stimulation, or development.

Dr. Lipton explains that one of the best moments of the day to listen to positive affirmation is **while we are falling asleep**, due to the fact that we are in the same vibration as when we are being hypnotized.

Nowadays, you can find numerous audio clips on YouTube with positive affirmations that you can listen to while falling asleep. If you are like me and need full silence to fall asleep, just play the clip for 30 minutes and then turn it off.

You will find that when you wake up the next morning, you will feel more confident when doing your Morning Zen. You'll avoid negative thoughts and will therefore feel less worried about the outside world. Though you are already working on your unconscious state of mind while doing Morning Zen, listening to positive affirmations while sleeping will help.

Another great tip is to use an app that sends you positive messages throughout the day. For example, can you remember a day when you were in a good mood and, from out of the blue, you received a message containing bad news or a problem to be resolved, making you feel helpless? And from there, your mind started creating all these concerns, your body entered stress mode, and your mood changed in a second?

Well, the good news is that we can also do the opposite. Instead of receiving bad news, you can receive positive messages. How? It can happen with the help of an app called *I Am Daily Affirmations*.

Its objective is to send you messages randomly throughout the day. Rather than news, status updates, or pending issues to resolve, they are positive affirmations with different topics like personal growth, work and career, health, relationships, happiness, etc.

As a result, your body receives little peaks of positivity, raising your self-esteem. Most messages like this are always welcome, and we all appreciate them. As the

Buddha famously said, "We are what we think," meaning the mind is everything. What you think, you become, so put fill your mind with positive messages.

The basic app is completely free, but if you want to unlock other features, you have to enroll in a premium subscription. I fully recommend it because it helps reduce negative self-talk, gives inspiration, motivation, confidence, and puts you in a better mood. And while I like to use *I Am*, if you prefer another one with a similar purpose, you are welcome to do so.

Along with the habits I have mentioned, there are numerous things that we can do to improve ourselves every day. And if we learn something new, work on our mood and attitude, and put it all into practice every day, we will definitely enjoy life more than we used to.

Now, if you are ready to incorporate the last habit into your Morning Zen, the third habit of the third block, jump to the next chapter, which is sure to delight you.

CHAPTER 20

THE MOVEMENT

Morning Zen

Adrian Gonzalez

Instagram: @the_morning_zen

CHAPTER 20

THE MOVEMENT

After reading your Manifesto while enjoying your coffee or morning drink and then using the Five Breathing Elements to energize your attitude, you will end your Morning Zen with this final step, called the Movement.

The Movement is like your final signature to tell the universe that you are ready to start your day. In other words, when you do it, you are telling your mind and body that it's time to jump into combat; the war is on. It works perfectly as a final call to tell yourself that Morning Zen is about to wrap up.

In popular action movies, it's common for the main character or fighter to make a final movement or gesture that puts him in warrior or invincible mode. One great example is the classic movie with Sylvester Stallone called *Over the Top*. In the movie, Sylvester plays a trucker who decides to mend his relationship with his son after his wife dies. He also participates in arm-wrestling tournaments to make money to help rebuild his life. Maybe you remember this movie because of its soundtrack, which had a hit by Kenny Loggins, "Meet Me Half Way."

Lincoln Hawk, the character played by Stallone, has a final movement before he enters warrior mode: when he is about to compete, he slowly turns his cap around and makes a little change to his hand grip. These two small actions energize and fortify him, and you can guess what happens next. Yes, he defeats his adversary. In the movie, Lincoln calls it "a switch." We call it the **Movement**.

Another great example of this can be found in Bruce Lee movies. When he's fighting an opponent and seems about to lose, he gets hit or cut, which causes him to start bleeding. Then it happens: he takes his fingers and smears them with his blood. Next, he rubs his fingers together and tastes his own blood. And then something happens. Well, that is the Movement, meaning you instantly know that Bruce Lee has entered anger mode.

This makes him sharper in his attack and is a sign that Bruce Lee is about to defeat his opponent.

Putting it in our real life. If you are like me and enjoy watching documentaries more than fictional series, you might have seen one about Tony Robbins called *I Am Not Your Guru*. It was filmed behind the scenes of the event called "Date with Destiny," which took place in Boca Raton, Florida. Among other things, the documentary shows Tony doing his own special movement.

Every time he is about to go out on stage to start an event, a few seconds before, he does a particular movement similar to the ones mentioned above. It consists of a mix of moves. First, he moves his legs combined with little jumps. At the same time, he does a whip while clenches his other fist pounding hard against his chest. To finish, he does a quick spin, plus a **power pose**, and once he completes that, he totally enters a state of mind where he is ready to rock. When watching him do it, you can sense that it helps him become energized and confident.

My point in telling you all this is that you should develop your own Movement before going to war. And by war, I mean the rest of your day. This Movement, as I said before, is personal, meaning you can do whatever you want. If you need help coming up with something, though, here are some recommendations for how to create one. Begin with a big inhalation, hold your breath, and then use a mix of various motions.

Try to include your arms or hands. From there, you can add whatever you like. Try to do these moves so that they flow together. The Movement should only last about three to five seconds, and finish with a big exhalation of the breath you've been holding.

Remember to keep it simple so you can easily repeat it every day as part of that ultimate step of your Morning Zen. And with the previous examples, this Movement should make you feel energized once you finish it, so when you do it, do it with the concentration of a ritual before a battle.

Now, if you would like to practice it right now, go and take a few minutes to develop it, or just go with the flow every time you finish Morning Zen until you've developed and fine-tuned it.

Once you have read the Five Breath Elements for your attitude, execute your natural, energized, flowy Movement. Finish the Movement with an exhalation and call it a Morning Zen. Yes, you have finished it.

Now you have welcomed the day, shouting to the world that you are good to go. So, reply to all your messages and feel free to check your emails and interact with the outside world.

Practicing Morning Zen will make you feel better, invigorated, and you will notice that life conspires for you and on your behalf. This means that you will fight to accomplish your Manifesto. You will notice a happier morning because of your gratitude and the good music. You will notice order and the neat bed you have made. You will notice that the things you wrote down in your intentions are starting to happen. You will be ready for your meetings because of your positive attitude and review of your day. You will feel less tired because you woke up with no alarm. You will notice that with the Morning Concoction and Meditation practice, you are working on your health. You will find a new perspective on life.

And you will do all of this and more, simply by reprogramming the first few minutes of your day, meaning you will empower your life by transforming your mornings.

As I mentioned at the beginning of this book, success for you now has a new meaning, and that is to be satisfied by accomplishing all the steps of Morning Zen, which are under your control. By seamlessly following this Zen routine, you will feel that you can eat the world and anything is possible. And with every day that passes, you will be more convinced of this. Remember, success is the ability to comply with the training, routines, or tasks under our control.

People will connect with Morning Zen in different ways. The beauty of this world lies in the divergence and variety of its people, and we all have different tastes, points of view, thoughts, and goals. This is what makes the world rich. Hopefully, some habits in Morning Zen will soon feel indispensable for your mornings. When you discover this, you will understand that you haven't just invested in a book, but in your happier life.

In the end, Morning Zen is for you, for your personal enhancement to build strength and a positive attitude. Now that I've shared it with you, it's time to show yourself that these new amazing behaviors can be performed by you and for you.

To resume, here are the steps to follow with Morning Zen: place your digital clock in front of your bed; wake up with no alarm; go to the kitchen and prepare your Morning Concoction; return to your room to meditate; write down your gratitude and intentions; play your Happy

Healthy Music; make your bed; sing and dance a little; shower; review your day and your meetings; put on your "fresh to death clothes"; after breakfast, enjoy your morning drink in the company of your Manifesto, reenergize your attitude with the Five Breath Elements; and close it with your personal Movement. Now you are ready to connect with the outside world and win the day's battle.

The secret of Morning Zen is that it can be adapted to your needs. And like composers or musicians say, once a song is released to the world, it no longer belongs to them; rather, it belongs to the world and to each person who identifies with that song. The same is true for Morning Zen. Once you begin to practice it, **you will feel that it belongs more to you than to me**. And that is the idea, to make it feel like it is yours, your Morning Zen.

Enjoy this gift of making yourself better each day. You searched for it, you found it, you deserve it. So, enjoy your life and enjoy your Morning Zen.

Thanks,

Adrian Antonio Gonzalez

THE END

ACKNOWLEDGEMENTS

I would like to thank Mrs. Luisa De Hoyos, who fought for me when I was little so I could go to a bilingual school and learn the beautiful language called English. Over the years, I have earned a bachelor's degree in engineering, upgraded into a master's in business administration. I have taken numerous courses and seminars in HR, marketing, and design, but few of these subjects have contributed as much to my success as English. Learning English has opened more doors and connections for me than I ever thought possible, And I will always be thankful that my parents put me in a good bilingual elementary school.

I would like to thank Vita for all her advice and her constant suggestion to "grab a book and read." This phrase was repeated several times during my childhood and never clicked, but sometimes good messages can take years to arrive—if not, ask NASA—and the same happened to me. It finally landed in that place called "my brain," and I began to read and develop an understanding of how good books use rhythm and entertain readers. As a result, I wrote this book.

I would like to thank all my English teachers in Instituto Panamericano and my former boss Gina Cano, who used the excuse that she understands Spanish but prefers not to speak it to help me develop my English skills. If you have kids, please put them in a bilingual school. Good things will come from it. By the way, Gina thank you as well for your enormous feedback and advice on this project.

Also, I would like to thank my great friend Guillermo Oscar. Out of all my friends, he has done the most to support me on all my adventures and help me develop my ideas. Sometimes we need that person who will support us even though we do not know how the project will end. If you have that kind of friend, keep them close. They are the ones who give you that little pat on the back and believe more in your talent than you do.

I would like to thank my brother, Arkel Gonzalez, and his wife, Adriana Simion, who always helped me to crystallize and pushed me to finish this project.

Also, I'd like to give a big thanks to the great Panamanian writer Miguel Esteban Gonzalez, AKA Dj Q, who guided me through the process to come. He has written several horror novels that I wholeheartedly invite you to read.

I would also like to thank Jefferson and Kathy from FirstEditing.com, who put their final touch on this project. Also, Microsoft for Office 365 and OneDrive. Thank God I had everything in the cloud so I could continue this project when devices failed. Satya Nadella if you are reading this, my greetings.

To my great and savvy boss, Dr. Pedro Gonzalez Castillo, thank you for setting me on the right routes with my projects.

I will always be thankful to Eleonora Gabriele, the awesome headhunter who believed and put on the map this amazing project. And, I will never forget my good friend Mariya Andrianova, who has closely accompanied me all this way.

Thank you to Jorge and Jahir Singh, Ruben, Aura and Aixa Rodriguez, Alexandra, Valery, Juan Carlos Velasco, Mario Ardila, Nancy and Meylin Hernandez, Jorge Martinez, Sherina Mayani, Lincoln Mcloud, Rafa Zalabata, Caro Montoya, Lionel Brown, Maritza Sanchez, Uncle Esther, Yoly, Itzel, and all my family members who supported me, especially on the days I was doing laundry and used the time to write.

Thank you to my Argentinian friends, Juan Matin, Nicolas "Puma" Gismondi, Diego Balan, Sasha y Janson,

Daniel Muzzalupo, Hernan Basualdo, Gonzalo Zugazaga, Any Ayala, Carolina Wechselberger, Gaby Olivera, Andres Hatum and all my classmates and professors from IAE. I carry all of you in my heart.

I also want to thank Joanne Xholitana Gordon, Alejandro Abrego, Alexandra Rodriguez, Cita Solano for the support. My cousin Querube Rivera, who practice these routines in the raw way and have always been convinced of what a wonderful gift this project is. And thank you to those who inspired me with their habits, like Professor Arturo Lopez Malumbre, Rafa Pino Pinto, and Beto Domingo, who invited me to participate in further degree programs, and Kamala Marroquin, who introduced me to the practice of meditation.

To all my supporters and investors, I have nothing more to say than thank you for believing in me, this project, and the future to come.

Thank you to Dakota, who was always with me during this creative process, to Athens Pizza, Mentiritas Blancas, and Café Unido, the places where I was inspired to write, and to everyone in the office, including Doris, Roberto, Indira, Ismara, Toto, Jean, Jonathan, who were with me during this phase.

By the way, in case you visit Panama, and want to try

one of the best pizzas in town, please go to Athen's Pizza and you will delight a different and delicious flat type of pizza keeping all its crispness and tastefulness you can enjoy on this dish.

And last but not least, I want to thank my mom, who supported and cared for me at her place when I needed a home and the inspiration to start and finish this project. I love you, Mom.

And with that, there is nothing more to say than thank you, who have read this book and embarked on this powerful journey, hope you enjoyed it. In case you would like to know more about me, follow me in my Social's and future coachings to come. Thank you.

ABOUT THE AUTHOR

Adrian Gonzalez was born and raised in Panama. He worked for more than 10 years developing a mix between skills, habits, and disciplines, putting it all together into one concept, and with this he discovered all the amazing benefits that come from it. Then, he cracked the code by developing a seamless way it can be followed and performed by anyone, during the mornings. And from there he had helped several people, managers, CEOs, and entrepreneurs that were passing thru difficult times like bankruptcies, separation process and life plateau, making them appreciate a happier life, empower into their goals again and find out this new meaning of success.

Contents